Saint Joseph

CATECHISM FOR YOUNG CATHOLICS

Found to be in conformity with the *Catechism of the Catholic Church* by the Subcommittee on the Catechism, United States Conference of Catholic Bishops

No. 3

Grades 6, 7, and 8

CATHOLIC BOOK PUBLISHING CORP.
New Jersey

Dedicated to
SAINT JOSEPH
Patron of the Universal Church

Nihil Obstat: Rev. Pawel Tomczyk, Ph.D.
Censor Librorum

Imprimatur: ✠ Kevin J. Sweeney, D.D.
Bishop of Paterson

May 20, 2022

(T-232)

ISBN 978-1-953152-94-7

Printed in China 24 SH 2

catholicbookpublishing.com

FOREWORD

As the Catholic Church revitalizes the mission of teaching the Faith, the 2020 edition of the *Directory for Catechesis* provides clear guidance for catechesis and presents universal norms to assist both pastors and catechists in their evangelization efforts. The *Directory* underscores the close link between evangelization and catechesis.

In concert with the *Directory*, the Saint Joseph Catechism for Young Catholics series adheres to the presentation of the Catholic Faith—as expressed in the *Catechism of the Catholic Church*—as a touchpoint for teaching while emphasizing Scripture and being mindful of papal writings, such as Pope Francis' Apostolic Exhortation *Evangelii Gaudium* (EG).

Evangelii Gaudium expresses the importance of family in forming the faith of children. "The family is experiencing a profound cultural crisis, as are all communities and social bonds. In the case of the family, the weakening of these bonds is particularly serious because the family is the fundamental cell of society, where we learn to live with others despite our differences and to belong to one another; it is also the place where parents pass on the faith to their children" (EG 66).

Pope Francis continues: "Growing numbers of parents do not bring their children for baptism or teach them how to pray.... The causes of this breakdown include: a lack of opportunity for dialogue in families, the influence of the communications media, a relativistic subjectivism, unbridled consumerism which feeds the market, lack of pastoral care among the poor, the failure of our institutions to be welcoming, and our difficulty in restoring a mystical adherence to the faith in a pluralistic religious landscape" (EG 70).

The four volumes in the Saint Joseph Catechism for Young Catholics series endeavor to assist parents in the spiritual formation of their children. Using an effective Question-and-Answer format, the essential elements of Catholic doctrine are presented in an orderly way in all four books, so children can easily retain them with greater understanding. It may even be possible that parents will reacquaint themselves with certain fundamentals of the Faith as they work with their children. What a wonderful opportunity to share God's truths within the closeness, caring, and love of family.

Catholic Book Publishing Corp.

PRAYER BEFORE INSTRUCTION

Come, Holy Spirit, fill the hearts of your faithful and enkindle in them the fire of your love.

℣. Send forth your Spirit and they shall be created.

℟. **And you shall renew the face of the earth.**

Let us pray. O God, who have taught the hearts of your faithful people by sending them the light of your Holy Spirit, grant us by the same Spirit to have a right judgment in all things and evermore to rejoice in his holy comfort. Through Christ our Lord. Amen.

PRAYER AFTER INSTRUCTION

Jesus, I come to you. You are the Way that I want to follow in obedience to your commandments, your counsels, and your example. Let me walk after you in the way of obedience, self-denial, and sacrifice, which leads to heaven and to you.

Jesus, you are the Truth. You are "the Light which enlightens everyone who comes into this world." I believe in your Gospel. I want to know you that I may love you.

Jesus, you are the Life, through your sanctifying grace, which is the life of our souls; through your words, which are "the living bread which has come down from heaven"; through your Heart, which is the fountain of life for individual souls and for society.

I cling to your word with all my heart. I hunger for the living bread of your Eucharist. I open my heart eagerly to the life-giving streams from Your Sacred Heart. I unite myself inwardly to all its intentions. May this divine Heart reign universally, over the children of the Church and over all humanity. Amen.

CONTENTS

Part Five
THE CHURCH

Part Six
THE SACRAMENTS

Part Seven
SIN

Part Eight
THE LIFE OF GRACE

Part Nine
THE MORAL LIFE

Part Ten
MARY AND THE SAINTS

Part Eleven
DEATH, JUDGMENT, ETERNITY

Abbreviations

CCC Catechism of the Catholic Church

UR Unitatis Redintegratio (Vatican II Decree on Ecumenism)

The Holy Trinity

Part One — THE MYSTERY OF ONE GOD

CHAPTER 1 The Holy Trinity

1. What is the history of salvation?

The history of salvation is the story of God's dealing with man.

The history of salvation tells us how God saved us. It is the plan by which God—the Father, the Son, the Holy Spirit—revealed himself to man, made peace between God and man by his Death on the Cross, and united with himself those turned away from sin.

2. How did God deal with man?

God dealt with man by (1) revealing himself to man and (2) saving man from sin.

(1) God made himself known to people. Revelation means that God showed us something of himself. He made himself known to us that he might save us. The Bible tells us about this revelation. The Bible is the written record of God's actions in the world. It is true because it is God's own word, which he made known to the writers of the Bible.

(2) Choosing sin, we lost God's life. God sent his Son to save us from sin and death and to give us God's life of grace. Because of his Son God now forgives our sins if we are truly sorry and if we want to be his friends.

3. How did God reveal himself in the Old Testament?

God revealed himself in the Old Testament as the one true personal God and prepared to reveal the Trinity later.

In the Old Testament of the Bible we read about God showing himself to us as the one true personal God. People learned that God was real, that he was faithful to his promises, and that people could be his friends if they put their trust in him.

4. What is the mystery of the Trinity?

The mystery of the Trinity is the one true God in three Persons—the Father, the Son, and the Holy Spirit.

Jesus Christ has revealed to us the secrets of the kingdom of heaven. The greatest of his teachings is the secret of God himself. He has told us of the life of God. Jesus taught us that in the one God there are three Persons, each equal to each other. He told us the names of these three Divine Persons: Father, Son, and Holy Spirit.

God has revealed this mystery to us because he wants us to know him as he is, to know as much about him as we can so that we might love him more in return for his boundless love for us.

5. How was the mystery of the Trinity expressed in the New Testament?

The mystery of the Trinity was expressed in the person, words, and actions of Jesus Christ.

After speaking through the prophets, God sent his Son. He came among people in the Person of his Son, Jesus Christ. Jesus told us the "Good News" of salvation. This message is found in the New Testament. By his words and actions, and especially in his holy Person, Jesus made known the deepest truths about God. The Blessed Trinity is the deepest of all mysteries.

6. How did Jesus Christ reveal himself?

Jesus Christ revealed himself as the eternal and divine Son of God.

Jesus said that he is the Son, the Only Begotten Son of the Father, equal to the Father.

Speaking of himself, Jesus said, "For God so loved the world that he gave his only Son, so that everyone who believes in him may not perish but may attain eternal life" (Jn 3:16).

At the Last Supper he prayed to the Father, "Father, the hour has come. Glorify your Son, so that your Son may glorify you, since you have given him authority over all people, so that he may give eternal life to all those you have given him. . . . So now, Father, glorify me in your presence with the glory I had with you before the world began" (Jn 17:1-2, 5).

Jesus said to his apostles, "Everything that the Father has is mine" (Jn 16:15).

Philip once said, "Lord, show us the Father." Jesus answered, "Have I been with you all this time, Philip, and you still do not know me? Whoever has seen me has seen the Father. How can you say, 'Show us the Father'? Do you not believe that I am in the Father and the Father is in me?" (Jn 14:8-10).

7. Did Jesus reveal the Father?

Jesus more fully revealed the Father.

Jesus constantly spoke of his Father, calling him always by that name. When he drove the money changers from the temple, he said, "Stop turning my Father's house into a marketplace!" (Jn 2:16).

Jesus said to his apostles, "By this is my Father glorified, that you bear much fruit and become my disciples. As the Father has loved me, so have I loved you. Remain in my love" (Jn 15:8-9).

Jesus taught us to love our heavenly Father because he loves us and wants to help us in all the needs of our body and soul. He wants to bring his children to his heavenly home.

8. Did Jesus reveal the Holy Spirit?

Jesus revealed the third Divine Person, the Holy Spirit, whom the Father and he, as the Risen Lord, sent to his Church.

Jesus promised to send a third Divine Person, the equal of himself and the Father.

At the Last Supper he told the apostles, "I will ask the Father, and he will give you another Advocate to be with you forever, the Spirit of Truth whom the world cannot accept because it neither sees him nor knows him. But you know him, because he dwells with you and will be in you" (Jn 14:16).

"The Advocate, the Holy Spirit, whom the Father will send in my name, will teach you everything and remind you of all that I have said to you" (Jn 14:26).

"When the Advocate comes whom I will send you from the Father, the Spirit of Truth who comes from the Father, he will testify on my behalf" (Jn 15:26).

9. What did Jesus, the Divine Teacher, teach his disciples?

The Divine Teacher (1) taught his disciples about the true God and (2) called them to become children of God through the gift of the Spirit.

(1) Since he was God, Jesus could teach us about the true God. He told his apostles that he is the way to the Father. By getting to know him they get to know the Father also. They can see the love of the Father in the actions of Jesus, because Jesus said that he and his Father are one.

When he sent his apostles to preach the Gospel to the whole world, Jesus told them to baptize "in the name of the Father, and of the Son, and of the Holy Spirit" (Mt 28:19). Here Jesus expresses the idea of "one God in three persons, the 'consubstantial Trinity'" (Father, Son, and Holy Spirit) (CCC 253). "Inseparable in what they are, the divine persons are also inseparable in what they do" (CCC 267).

(2) Jesus called us to become children of God. We become children of God through a new life which he gives us. It is God's own life, given to us by the Holy Spirit. It is called "grace." Because he was the Son of God Jesus was able to give us a share of God's life and make us children of God. He does this through the gift of the Holy Spirit which he gives us.

10. How do we honor the Blessed Trinity?

We honor the Blessed Trinity by trying to (1) remember the presence of God the Father, Son, and Holy Spirit in our soul and (2) understand, as much as we can through faith, that through Baptism we are called to a close union of love with the three Divine Persons.

(1) We show our love for the Blessed Trinity when we remember that the Father, Son, and Holy Spirit are in our soul when we are in the state of grace. Jesus said, "Whoever loves me will keep my word, and my Father will love him, and we will come to him and make our abode with him" (Jn 14:23). "I will ask the Father, and he will give you another Advocate to be with you forever" (Jn 14:16).

We show our love for the Blessed Trinity when we pray to God. We may pray simply to God—to the Blessed Trinity. We may pray to any one of the three Divine Persons. We may pray as the Church does most often—to the Father, through the Son, in union with the Holy Spirit. Jesus said, "If you ask the Father for anything in my name, he will give it to you" (Jn 16:23).

(2) God lives in our soul by grace. We first received this grace through Baptism. Faith tells us that we are called to a close union of love with the Father, the Son, and the Holy Spirit. We belong to God who is closest to us. God is our Father; Jesus Christ is our Lord and Savior; the Holy Spirit is our teacher and guide.

A. FILL IN THE BLANKS

(The numeral at the end of each sentence shows which question gives the answer. These answers should be written out on a separate sheet of paper as homework or they can be discussed with the class.)

1. The history of salvation is.. (1)
2. God dealt with man by (1) ....and (2) ....(2)
3. God revealed himself in the Old Testament as .... (3)
4. The mystery of the Trinity is... (4)
5. Jesus Christ revealed himself as .... (6)
6. Jesus revealed the third Divine Person, the Holy Spirit, whom .... sent to his Church. (8)
7. Jesus taught his disciples about .... (9)
8. Jesus called his disciples and us to become .... (9)
9. We honor the Blessed Trinity by .... (10)
10. Through Baptism we are called to .... (10)

B. BIBLE READING

Exodus 3:4-14; 5:1-2

The Burning Bush

One day Moses, while leading the sheep of his father-in-law near a mountain, was startled by the sight of a bush on fire. He wondered why it did not burn up. He came closer to look at it, and he heard his name called by the voice of God. The voice told Moses to take off his sandals, for the place was holy.

From the bush God spoke to Moses: "I have seen the misery of my people in Egypt. I know about their sufferings. I have come down to free them and to lead them to a land flowing with milk and honey. I send you to Pharaoh. Lead my people, the Israelites, from Egypt."

Then God said to Moses, "You will say to the children of Israel, I AM sent me to you." This is the title with which I will be remembered from one generation to the next."

Moses and Aaron went to ask Pharaoh, king of Egypt, in the name of the LORD, to let the Israelites go to sacrifice in the desert.

Pharaoh answered, "Who is the LORD that I should listen to his voice and let Israel leave? I do not know the LORD, and I will not let Israel leave."

Discussion:

1. Why was Moses startled?
2. What did God say to Moses?
3. What name did God give himself?
4. Who helped Moses when he went before the king of Egypt?
5. What did Moses and Aaron ask the king to do?
6. Did the king do what they asked?

C. PRACTICE

1. Think of the Father, Son, and Holy Spirit dwelling in your soul by saying a short prayer like the Glory Be.
2. Make the Sign of the Cross very carefully.

We offer ourselves to God through Jesus

CHAPTER

2 True Worship of God

11. What must we believe about God?

We must believe that God is all-good, all-just, all-merciful, all-wise, all-perfect, and all-holy.

God is all-good. He is Love itself. He has given us all the good things we have because he loves us. He created the world to show forth his glory and to share his happiness with the beings he created. He shares his life with them. He loves all people and wills that all people be saved.

God is all-just. He promised to reward those who do good and to punish those who do evil.

God is all-merciful, ready to forgive any sinner who is truly sorry and who wishes to lead a good life.

God is all-wise. He knows all things, past, present, and future, even our secret thoughts, words, and actions. Nothing can be hidden from him.

God is all-perfect. He is all-holy because he is God. He is infinite because there is no limit to his life. He is eternal because he had no beginning and will have no end. He is all-powerful because he can do all things. He is everywhere.

God is the one limitless, almighty, all-knowing spirit. He does not need anything or anyone outside of himself. All things depend on him. Yet God cares for all things which he has created. He calls all people to become his adopted children.

12. How has God shown his love for us?

God has shown his love for us by (1) making firm promises to us and drawing us to himself by solemn agreements, (2) freeing and saving us, and (3) loving each of us with the love of a father and always caring for us.

(1) After our first parents, Adam and Eve, sinned, God made a promise to save all people. He kept his promise. He chose Abraham's descendants to be his own special people. With the help of Moses the Jewish people made a contract with God, called the "Covenant." God made known his will in the Ten Commandments. Though Israel broke the Covenant, God did not forsake his people. At last he came among his people in the person of his Son. A New Covenant was made in his Blood by his Death on the Cross.

(2) Through Jesus Christ God shows his love for us. He made known to us his loving plan of salvation. Now he even shares his life with us through Jesus. Through the suffering, Death, and Resurrection of Jesus we have received grace and God's life. Through him we have hope of eternal life with God in heaven.

(3) God truly loves us and takes care of us as a loving Father. He has made us his children through baptism and has prepared his heavenly kingdom to be our eternal home.

13. What should the thought of God's goodness do for us?

The thought of God's goodness should (1) make us find joy in the God who gives us eternal hope and (2) prompt us to worship him.

(1) We belong to God. He loves us and asks that we love him so that we may be with him forever in heaven. God's love for us should make us trust him and find our joy in him.

(2) We owe God loving service and worship. We show our loving service by obedience to his will. We worship him by our love and adoration.

14. How do we worship God?

We worship God by (1) offering ourselves to him through our Lord Jesus Christ, especially in the sacred liturgy, (2) doing his will in all our actions, and (3) using well the talents he has given us.

(1) We worship God especially when we adore him in the Holy Sacrifice of the Mass. We offer ourselves to him with the offering of Jesus. We worship God also when we pray to him.

(2) We worship God when we do his will by keeping his commandments as obedient children.

(3) We are in this world to know God, to love and serve him, and to use our talents in his service.

15. What should we hope for from the goodness of God?

From the goodness of God, we hope to receive the grace we need to live a life of love for God and neighbor for his glory.

We trust that God will help us to live a life of love for him and others. We live a life of love when we devote ourselves to our Creator. God will give us his help to love him as he wants us to love him. Our life can be very happy if only we open our hearts to him and try to use the graces he offers us each day to honor him and to help the people around us.

16. Why do many people today pay little attention to God?

Many people today pay little attention to God because modern life is taken up with things of the world rather than with God.

God continues to be good to us, and yet there are very many people in the world who hardly ever think of him; many even break his commandments. They are too interested in their own pleasures and in the things the world offers them.

We must accept God's word with deep faith and trust in his love for us, for he is faithful to his promises. But many people are not ready to believe in God.

17. Does everyone have some desire for God?

No matter how hidden, some desire for God is in the heart of everyone.

God has made us for himself, and we cannot find true happiness unless we look for it in him. Even when we do not want to think so, there is a secret desire in our hearts for God. Since God has helped us to know him more than many other people do, he expects us to love him more and serve him better. Our life will be blessed if we do so, and we can look forward to being with God forever in heaven.

A. FILL IN THE BLANKS

1. We must believe that God is all-good,......................................(11)
2. God has shown his love for us by (1) ...., (2) ...., and (3)......................................(12)
3. The thought of God's goodness should (1) .... and (2) ....(13)
4. We worship God by (1) ...., especially in the sacred liturgy, (2) doing his will in ...., and (3) using well ....(14)
5. From the goodness of God, we hope .... to live a life of .... (15)
6. Many people today pay little attention to God because ....(16)
7. No matter how hidden,..is in the heart of everyone. (17)

B. BIBLE READING

Genesis 22:1-18

The Test of Abraham

When Abraham was a hundred years old, Sarah, who was ninety, gave him a son. They called him "Isaac," meaning "laughter," for Sarah laughed to herself when she overheard the L*ORD tell Abraham that she would bear a son. Abraham and Sarah loved Isaac with all their hearts because he had been sent as God had promised.*

Some time later God tested Abraham. He said to him, "Abraham, Abraham!" He replied, "Here I am!" God said, "Take your son...and go to the land of Moriah and offer him as a burnt offering on the mountain that I will show you."

He began the journey accompanied by two servants and Isaac. On the third day, Abraham said to his servants, "Stay here. I and the boy will worship and then we will return to you."

Abraham took the wood they brought for the burnt offering and loaded it upon Isaac. He himself carried the fire and the knife. Isaac

asked, "Here are the fire and the wood, but where is the lamb for the burnt offering?"

Abraham answered, "God himself will provide the lamb for the burnt offering, my son!"

Arriving at the place of which God had spoken, Abraham built an altar and piled up the wood. He tied up Isaac and placed him on the altar so that he was lying upon the wood.

Then Abraham reached out and took the knife to kill his son. But the angel of the LORD called out from heaven and said, "Abraham! Abraham! Do not reach out your hand against the boy. Now I know that you fear God and you have not even withheld your son, your only son, from me."

Abraham looked up saw a ram that had its horns caught in a bush. He took the ram and offered it as a burnt offering instead of his son.

Then the angel told Abraham that because of his offering, God would bless him abundantly, he would have numerous descendants, and all the nations of the earth would be blessed through his descendants.

Discussion:

1. Why did God want to test Abraham?
2. How did Abraham worship God?
3. Why did the angel keep Abraham from killing his son?
4. Why is Isaac carrying the wood up the mountain a picture of Jesus our Savior?
5. Why did the heavenly Father let his own Son die on the Cross?
6. How did God reward Abraham for his love and obedience?

C. PRACTICE

1. Remember that it is your duty to worship God, especially on Saturday evening or on Sunday, the Lord's day. You worship God by offering the Holy Sacrifice of the Mass in his honor. Do this with all the love of your heart.
2. Be obedient to God no matter how hard it may be to obey him. Be obedient especially to your parents who have a right to tell you what you must do.

Part Two — CREATION

CHAPTER 3 The Beginning of the History of Salvation

18. What is creation?

Creation means that God made the whole universe out of nothing.

Creation is the way God gave life and the world to man. We owe all that we have to God. The Bible does not try to explain creation. God's people knew that he was Lord of life and the universe.

19. What did the action of God in the Old Testament show and prove?

The action of God in the Old Testament (1) showed his power and (2) proved that he is always with his people.

(1) In the Old Testament God's people learned the truth of God's almighty power in the creation.

(2) His power in creation reminded the people that God remains always with his people to protect and help them. His wonderful deeds of power and victory show that he kept his promises and that he loved his people.

20. What is the beginning of the mystery of salvation?

The creation of angels and of the world is the beginning of the mystery of salvation.

Long before God created man, he made the angels. They were spirits, meaning that they had no body. They had a brilliant mind to understand God's goodness and beauty; they had a free will to love and praise him. Some of the angels sinned and became evil spirits.

21. What is the first gift of God leading to Christ?

The creation of man is the first gift of God leading to Christ.

Man has a mind to know his Creator and a will to love him. To reach eternal happiness with God man must freely accept God's love and devote himself to his service. But Jesus is the one whom God sent to lead people to God. It is only through him that we can be saved. That is why we can say that the creation of man is the first gift of God leading to Christ.

22. Where is the all-powerful action of God for our salvation especially seen?

The all-powerful action of God for our salvation is especially seen in Christ's Resurrection from the dead.

Though he was made by God in a state of holiness, man turned against God of his own free will, being led to do so by the evil spirit. God sent his Son to free man from the slavery of sin and to make him holy again. He did this through the sufferings and Death of Jesus and through his glorious Resurrection. In this way God showed his all-powerful action for our salvation.

23. How should we look upon creation?

We should look upon creation as God's continuing action as he works out our salvation.

When we think of the creation of the angels, the world, and man, we should see how God's all-powerful action saved all of us. His great love for man led him to do so. The whole work of salvation receives its meaning from Jesus Christ, the incarnate Word. That work, beginning with the creation, showed itself in Christ's coming, his life on earth, his Death and Resurrection, and will show itself at his glorious Second Coming, which will complete the work of God.

24. How was God present in human history?

God was present in the history of Israel. He also was powerfully at work in the life, Death, and Resurrection of his Incarnate Son.

When we hear about the creation, we should not only think of God's act of making the world but also turn our mind to all that he did to save the people in this world. His deeds of salvation can be seen in the history of man and of the world, especially in the history of Israel. They lead to the most important events in our Lord's life, his Death and Resurrection.

25. How is God present among us today?

God is lovingly present in human history using his limitless power to help us. He will finish his saving work only at the end of the world.

The life, Death, and Resurrection of Jesus is the most important event of all time through which God shows himself and his love for man. He also shows himself in other events which are found in the Bible and in the life of the Church. God will continue to be present among us, showing his power and his love.

A. FILL IN THE BLANKS

1. Creation means that ....(18)

2. The action of God in the Old Testament (1) showed......................
.... and (2) proved that .... (19)

3. The creation .... is the beginning of the mystery of salvation. (20)

4. The ....is the first gift of God leading to Christ. (21)

5. The all-powerful action of God for our salvation is especially seen in ....(22)

6. We should look upon creation as..
as he works out .... (23)

7. God was present in .... He also was powerfully at work in .... of his Incarnate Son. (24)

8. God is lovingly present in human history using ....
.... He will finish his saving work only at ....(25)

B. BIBLE READING Genesis 1

God Created All Things

God had no beginning and he will have no end. He is eternal.

God made the angels. They are spirits like the soul of man. Lucifer was one of the most glorious and most beautiful of the angels. His name means "Bearer of Light." He became very proud and even wanted to be as great as God himself. He cried out against God, "I will not serve!" With him were other angels who also refused to obey God.

But the Archangel Michael cried out, "Who is like God?" Other good angels joined him in a great battle against Lucifer and his bad angels, and drove the bad ones into a place of eternal punishment. We call Lucifer "Satan," and his bad angels "devils."

To have a beautiful place for man to live, God made the universe.

God created all things.

On the first day God made earth out of nothing. Then God said, "Let there be light!" And there was light. God separated the light from the darkness. And he called the light day, and he called the darkness night.

On the second day God made the sky and called it the heavens.

On the third day God said, "Let the waters under the heavens be gathered into one place and let a dry place appear. Let the land bring forth plants and trees of every kind."

On the fourth day God made the sun, the moon, and the stars.

On the fifth day God made sea creatures to fill the waters. He created birds and other creatures that were to fly in the sky. God blessed them saying, "Be fruitful and multiply."

On the sixth day God said, "Let the earth bring forth living creatures each according to its kind.

And God said, "Let us make man in our image and likeness, and let them have dominion over every living creature." God formed man out of the dust of the earth and he breathed his breath of life into his nostrils and man became a living creature.

God blessed the seventh day and he consecrated it, for on it he rested from all the work he had done when he created all things.

Discussion:

1. Who are the angels?
2. How did the angels sin against God?
3. What did the Archangel Michael and the other good angels do?
4. What did God make on the first day? On the second day? On the third day? On the fourth day? On the fifth day? On the sixth day? What happened on the seventh day?

C. PRACTICE

1. Everything in the world was created to give glory to God. We, the greatest of all his earthly creatures, must praise God and love him with all our hearts. We should thank him for the beautiful things we see around us. Our greatest thanksgiving is Holy Mass.
2. Often during the day say a little prayer to thank God for the good things you receive from him. Thank God in the beautiful prayer: Glory be to the Father, and to the Son, and to the Holy Spirit. As it was in the beginning, is now, and ever shall be, world without end. Amen.

CHAPTER 4 Knowledge of God and the Witness of Christian Love

26. Can man come to know God through created things?

(1) Sacred Scripture says that man can come to know God through the things God has made. (2) The Church teaches that man can come to know God as the beginning and end of all that is from thinking about created things.

(1) The God who loves us makes himself known to us in various ways. He teaches us through the things he has made. The Bible tells us that man can come to know him through the things he made.

(2) The Church also teaches that created things around us help us to see that the one who made them is God and that he can do all things. If we really love God, we will try to learn as much as we can about him, even from the things he made.

27. How can we help unbelievers to find God?

We can help unbelievers to find God by the witness of a life of (1) firm faith in God, (2) personal love of Christ, and (3) goodness and love.

(1) We can help people to turn to God if we give them a good example of our own deep faith in God.

(2) If people see our love for Christ in our good deeds, they will be moved to love him also.

(3) God has willed that all of us should make up one family and treat one another in a spirit of mutual respect, for all of us are called to the same goal—God himself. By our love for one another for the love of God and by other good works, we can help those who do not believe in God to find him.

28. What is our duty toward the world?

Faith in God and union with Christ also mean that we must help others to solve their problems as much as we can.

We show our love for God also by loving our neighbor—the people around us. Love for our neighbor makes us do all we can to help those who need our help and make the world better.

A. FILL IN THE BLANKS

1. Sacred Scripture says .... through the things God has made. (26)
2. The Church teaches that man can come to know God as the beginning and end of all that is from ....(26)
3. We can help unbelievers to find God by the witness of a life of (1) ...., (2) ...., and (3) .... (27)
4. Faith in God and union with Christ also mean that we must help others to ....(28)

B. BIBLE READING

1 Samuel 17:1-51

David and Goliath

At one time, the Philistines stood on one side of a mountain, and the Israelites stood on the mountainside facing them.

Out of the Philistines' camp came their champion, a ten-foot man named Goliath. He was covered with bronze armor. He called out to the Israelites, "Choose a man and have him come down to me. If he is able to fight me and kill me, then we will become your slaves. But if I defeat and kill him, then you will be our slaves and serve us."

King Saul and the Israelites were terrified. Over forty days passed. Still no Israelite dared to fight Goliath. One day David arrived at the Israelite camp to give food to his three brothers and others in Saul's army. He heard Goliath taunting the Israelites.

David asked, "Who is this uncircumcised Philistine that he should defy the armies of the living God?" He said to Saul, "Your servant will go out and fight with this Philistine."

Saul said to David, "You cannot go out against the Philistine. You are only a boy and he has been a warrior since he was young."

David replied, "Your servant has killed lion and bear. The LORD who has delivered me from the paw of the lion and the paw of the bear will deliver me out of the hands of this Philistine."

He took his staff in his hand, and he chose five smooth stones from out of the stream. With his sling in hand, he approached the Philistine.

The Philistine drew nearer to David, his shield-bearer preceding him. The Philistine held him in contempt for he was only a youth. Goliath said, "Am I a dog, that you come out to me with sticks? Come over to me, and I will give your flesh to the birds."

David said, "You are coming against me with sword, spear, and javelin. I am coming against you in the name of the LORD of hosts. The LORD will deliver you into my hands today."

David reached into his bag and pulled out a stone. He launched it with the sling and struck the Philistine on his forehead. He fell face first to the earth. David took Goliath's sword, killed him, and cut off his head with it.

Discussion:

1. Why was David not afraid to fight the giant?
2. What did David say to Goliath before he killed him?
3. How did David kill Goliath?
4. How did David give a good example to the godless Philistines?

C. PRACTICE

1. When you see the fields and lakes, flowers and animals, the stars in the sky, think of God who created them all to let you know more about himself. Make an act of love when you see God's goodness.
2. Try to help others to turn to God by coming to Mass faithfully and by being kind to people.
3. Pray that people who do not know God may come to know him.

THE BIBLE. . .

They devoted themselves to the teaching of the apostles and to the communal fellowship, to the breaking of bread and to prayers. A sense of awe was felt by all, for many wonders and signs were performed by the apostles. All the believers were together and owned everything in common. They would sell their property and possessions and distribute the proceeds to all according to what each one needed. Every day, united in spirit, they would assemble together in the temple. They would break bread in their homes and share their food with joyful and generous hearts as they praised God, and they were regarded with favor by all the people. And day by day the Lord added to those who were being saved. (Acts 2:42-47)

Ever since the creation of the world the invisible attributes of God's eternal power and divine nature have been clearly understood and perceived through the things he has made. Therefore, the conduct of these people is inexcusable. (Rom 1:20)

The heavens proclaim the glory of God; the firmament shows forth the work of his hands. (Ps 19:2)

Petitions to Jesus

O good Jesus: Word of the Eternal Father, convert me.
Son of Mary, take me as her child.
My Master, teach me.
Prince of Peace, give me peace.
My Refuge, receive me.
My Shepherd, feed my soul.
Model of patience, comfort me.

Meek and humble of Heart, help me to become like you.
My Redeemer, save me.
My God and my All, possess me.
The true Way, direct me.
Eternal Truth, instruct me.

Life of the saints, make me live in you.
My Support, strengthen me.
My Justice, justify me.
My Mediator with your Father, reconcile me.
Physician of my soul, heal me.
My Judge, pardon me.
My King, rule me.
My Sanctification, sanctify me.
Abyss of goodness, pardon me.

Living Bread from Heaven, nourish me.
Father of the prodigal, receive me.
Joy of my soul, be my only happiness.
My Helper, assist me.
My Protector, defend me.
My Hope, sustain me.
Object of my love, refresh me.
My Divine Victim, atone for me.
My Last End, let me possess You.
My Glory, glorify me. Amen.

Jesus, the Way, the Truth, and the Life

CHAPTER 5 Jesus Christ, Son of God, the Firstborn of All Creation, and Savior

29. What is the greatest of God's works?

The greatest of God's works is the taking on of human flesh by his Son, Jesus Christ, and this is called the Incarnation.

The greatest of God's works is the Incarnation of his Son, Jesus Christ. The Incarnation means that the Second Person of the Blessed Trinity, the Son of God, the Divine Word, became man and came to live among us.

30. Why did the Son come on earth?

The Son came on earth to (1) bring the world his own divine life, (2) save it from sin, and (3) make the world new again from within.

(1) Born of the Virgin Mary, the Son of God has truly been made one of us, like us in all things except sin. The human race lost God's life of grace through sin, the sin of our first parents. Because of his love for us Jesus brought grace back to us by his life, Death, and Resurrection. He showed us what it means to be a child of God.

(2) Jesus offered his life as the highest gift to his Father by dying on the Cross for us. In this way he redeemed the world. The Passion and Death of our Lord teach us the great evil of sin. It was

sin that caused him to suffer so much and to die. But he took away our sins and made us free to serve God and to reach heaven.

(3) Jesus showed us how we must belong to God. His whole life was devoted to doing the work and will of his Father. To receive God's life we must accept Jesus and his way of life. We do this through Baptism. Through the Catholic Church and its truth and sacraments we are able to keep this life in our soul. With this grace we can be united with God in this world and forever in heaven. Through his grace Jesus is for us a source of life and salvation from sin. In this way he renews the world from within.

31. Why is Jesus Christ called the Firstborn of all creation?

Jesus Christ is the Firstborn of all creation because he is before all—all things have been created in him, through him, and for him.

"He is the image of the invisible God, the firstborn of all creation" (Col 1:15). This perfect image of God is the firstborn in the order of creation because Christ is the most excellent of all creatures as well as their Creator.

32. How was Jesus Christ made known to us as God's Son in power?

Through his Resurrection Jesus was made known to us as God's Son in power, for he was obedient unto death and exalted as Lord of all.

God chose his Son to be the one to suffer and to die for our sins. Because of his obedience he was raised up as Lord of all. By conquering death through his own power in his Resurrection, Jesus has shown himself Master of life and death. Therefore he is true God and true man, our Savior.

33. What has Jesus Christ done for us through his Resurrection?

Being the Firstborn of the dead, Jesus Christ (1) gives eternal life to all, and (2) in him we are made anew.

(1) When Christ passed from death to life he brought about our passing from the death of sin to life in him.

(2) We receive the new life of grace in Baptism because in Christ we are created anew. We are now God's children. St. Peter says, "Blessed be the God and Father of our Lord Jesus Christ. In his great mercy he has given us a new birth to a living hope through the Resurrection of Jesus Christ from the dead and to an inheritance that is . . . reserved in heaven for you" (1 Pet 1:3-4).

34. Why is Jesus Christ our Savior?

Jesus Christ is our Savior because through him all creatures will be saved from the slavery of sin.

St. Paul speaks of sin as a slavery. Jesus is our Savior because he saved us from sin.

35. Is there any other Savior?

There is no salvation in anyone but Jesus Christ, nor has there ever been.

All stand in need of Christ, their Savior, for by his own power no one is freed from the slavery of sin. Scripture says, "There is no salvation in anyone else" (Acts 4:12).

The Birth of Jesus

A. FILL IN THE BLANKS

1. The greatest of God's works is .... and this is called the ....(29)

2. The Son came on earth to (1) ...., (2) save it ...., and (3) make the world...................... (30)

3. Jesus Christ is the Firstborn of all creation because ....—all things have been created .... him, ... him, and.......... him. (31)

4. Through his .... Jesus was made known to us as ...., for he was .... and ....(32)

5. Being the Firstborn of the dead, Jesus Christ (1) gives ...., and (2) in him .... (33)

6. Jesus Christ is our Savior because through him .... of sin. (34)

7. There is no salvation in anyone but ...., nor has there ever been. (35)

B. BIBLE READING

Matthew 1:20-21
Luke 2:1-7

The Birth of Jesus

Soon after Joseph learned that Mary was with child, an angel of the Lord appeared to him in a dream and said,"Joseph, son of David, do not be afraid to receive Mary into your home as your wife. For this child has been conceived in her womb through the Holy Spirit. She will give birth to a son, and you shall name him Jesus, for he will save his people from their sins."

After Joseph took Mary into his home, a decree was issued by Caesar Augustus that a census should be taken throughout the entire world.

Everyone traveled to his own town to be enrolled. Joseph therefore went from the town of Nazareth in Galilee to Judea, to the city of David called Bethlehem, because he was of the house and family of David.

While they were there, the time came for her to have her child, and she gave birth to her firstborn son. She wrapped him in swaddling clothes and laid him in a manger, because there was no room for them in the inn.

Discussion:

1. What did the angel tell Joseph in his dream?
2. Why did Joseph and Mary travel to Bethlehem?
3. To whose family did Joseph belong?
4. What did Mary do after Jesus was born?
5. What feast is celebrated in memory of the birth of our Lord?

C. PRACTICE

1. The prayer which reminds us of the scene of the Annunciation, the moment when God became man, is the "Hail Mary." This prayer contains the words of Scripture itself: the greeting of the angel to Mary and the greeting of her cousin Elizabeth to the Mother of God. We should say this prayer often every day.
2. When we receive Holy Communion, we receive the same Jesus who was made man for us—his Body and Blood, Soul and Divinity. We should try to love Jesus more through frequent reception of the Eucharist.

JESUS SPEAKS:

"Whoever has seen me has seen the Father. How can you say, 'Show us the Father'? Do you not believe that I am in the Father and the Father is in me?" (Jn 14:9-10)

"You have come to believe because you have seen me. Blessed are those who have not seen and yet have come to believe." (Jn 20:29)

CHAPTER 6 Jesus Christ, the Center of All God's Saving Works

36. What is God's plan for us?

The carrying out of God's plan for us is the story of man's salvation—to form his people into "the whole Christ."

Jesus Christ gave himself for us in his Passion that he might redeem us from sin and make us a people pleasing to God. He then sent the Holy Spirit, the spirit of adoption, to make us children of God. In this way he made in himself a new people, filled with the grace of God. United with Jesus, the new people of God are "the whole Christ." He offers them to his Father and gives him glory. This is the Father's plan for the salvation of all people.

37. Why is Jesus Christ the center of all God's saving works?

Christ is the center of all God's saving works because the Christian can fulfill his task of making creation give glory to God through the power of Jesus the Savior.

Jesus Christ became man so that as perfect man he might save all people and sum up all things in himself. He summed up in himself the mysteries of our salvation by his Death and Resurrection; he received all power in heaven and on earth; he founded his Church as a means of our salvation. So in Christ, our Redeemer, we are joined to all others.

Since Christ is the center of all God's works of salvation, through him we can make all creation give glory to God. All this was made possible through his love and power. God is the full meaning of life, and Jesus is the way to God. Jesus asks us to believe in him, put our hope in him for the future, and to love him with all our heart. Jesus said, "The Father loves the Son, and he has entrusted everything into his hand. Whoever believes in the Son has eternal life" (Jn 3:35-36).

A. FILL IN THE BLANKS

1. The carrying out of God's plan for us is ....(36)
2. The story of man's salvation is to ....(36)
3. Christ is the center of all God's saving works because .... through the power of .... (37)

B. BIBLE READING Matthew 17:1-10

The Transfiguration

One day, Jesus took Peter and James and his brother John and led them up a high mountain by themselves.

And in their presence he was transfigured; his face shone like the sun, and his clothes became dazzling white.

Suddenly, there appeared to them Moses and Elijah, conversing with him.

Then Peter said to Jesus,"Lord, it is good for us to be here. If you wish, I will make three tents here—one for you, one for Moses, and one for Elijah."

While he was still speaking, suddenly a bright cloud cast a shadow over them. Then a voice from the cloud said, "This is my beloved Son, with whom I am well pleased. Listen to him."

When the disciples heard this, they fell on their faces and were greatly frightened. But Jesus came and touched them, saying,"Stand up, and do not be frightened."

And when they raised their eyes, they saw no one, but only Jesus. As they were coming down from the mountain, Jesus commanded them, "Tell no one about this vision until the Son of Man has been raised from the dead."

Discussion:

1. Whom did Jesus take with him when he went up the mountain to pray?
2. What happened to Jesus on the mountain?
3. What did Peter say to Jesus?
4. What were the words of the heavenly Father?
5. What did Jesus say to his three apostles when they were frightened by the voice?
6. What did Jesus say to them when they were walking down the mountain?

C. PRACTICE

1. God's people worship him in the highest way in the Holy Sacrifice of the Mass. At the end of the Eucharistic Prayer, the priest says: "Through him [that is, through Christ], and with him, and in him, O God almighty Father, in the unity of the Holy Spirit, all glory and honor is yours, for ever and ever." And the people then acclaim, "Amen." At each Mass offer yourself to God through Jesus so that God may be praised.
2. Since Jesus is the center of all God's works of salvation, we should turn to him with great confidence in his love and power to help us to lead a good Christian life and to save our soul.

JESUS SPEAKS:

The Father loves the Son, and he has entrusted everything into his hand. Whoever believes in the Son has eternal life."

(Jn 3:35-36)

THE BIBLE . . .

It was he who established some as apostles, some as prophets, some as evangelists, and some as pastors and teachers, to equip the saints for the work of ministry in building up the body of Christ, until all of us attain to the unity of faith and the knowledge of the Son of God, to full maturity, as measured by the full stature of Christ. (Eph 4:11-13)

When all things are subjected to him, then the Son himself will also be subjected to the one who made all things subject to him, so that God may be all in all. (1 Cor 15:28)

Jesus told the high priest that He is the Son of God

CHAPTER 7

Jesus Christ, True God and True Man

38. Why is Jesus true God?

Jesus is true God because he is God's Only Begotten Son, and in him there is all fullness of divinity.

Jesus Christ is true God, the Son of the heavenly Father, the Divine Word of God made man. But he is only one Person, and that Person is the Second Person of the Blessed Trinity. St. John wrote, "In the beginning was the Word, and the Word was with God, and the Word was God" (Jn 1:1).

Jesus said he was God. He said to the Jews, "The very works that I am doing, testify about me, that the Father has sent me" (Jn 5:36). "I speak of what I have seen in my Father's presence" (Jn 8:38).

At the trial of Jesus the high priest said to him, "I command you to tell us before the living God whether you are the Christ, the Son of God." Jesus replied, "You have said it. But I tell you: From now on you will see the Son of Man seated at the right hand of the Power and coming on the clouds of heaven" (Mt 26:63-64).

The night before Jesus died he prayed, "Father, the hour has come. Glorify your Son, so that your Son may glorify you, since you have given him authority over all people, so that he may give eternal life to all those you have given him" (Jn 17:1-2).

39. How does the Creed express our faith in the divinity of Christ?

The Nicene Creed says of Jesus Christ: "God from God, Light from Light, true God from true God, begotten not made, consubstantial with the Father."

The chief teaching of the Catholic Church about Jesus Christ is that he is God made man. It is Jesus Christ the God-Man whom we see and hear in the Gospels and receive in the Eucharist. It is to him with the Father and the Holy Spirit that we pray: Glory be to the Father, and to the Son, and to the Holy Spirit.

40. Why is Jesus Christ true man?

Jesus Christ is true man because he, the Son of God, was "made visible in the flesh" (1 Tim 3:16). (1) As man, Jesus thought with a human mind, acted with a human heart. (2) Jesus joined himself with every human being except in sin.

(1) The Son of God became a real man, having real flesh, a human body and soul. He is a human being just as we are. He felt the joys and sorrows, pleasures and pains that we feel as humans. As man Jesus had a human mind and a human will to know and to love as we do. This means that he was born into this world and lived a real human life.

Mary was the Mother of Jesus. He was conceived by the Holy Spirit within her. Joseph was Mary's husband and acted as foster father to Jesus during childhood. Jesus died just as the rest of us must.

(2) Jesus joined himself with us in all things except sin. He is the all-holy God. The human nature he assumed never knew sin.

41. How did Jesus show his concern for people?

Jesus lived among people, was close to them, reached out to all—the virtuous and the sinner, the poor and the rich, especially the suffering.

Jesus was kind to all people and spent his life helping them in their needs. He traveled all over Israel, teaching the people about his Father and working miracles. His whole teaching was about loving God with our whole heart and our neighbor as ourselves. He loved especially the poor, the sick, and the troubled.

Jesus loved sinners and forgave their sins. He offered his life to save all mankind.

42. What do we see in Christ's concern for people?

In Christ's concern for people we see God's love for us all.

We cannot see God, but when God sent his Son to live among us and to save us by his Death on the Cross, we can see how much God really loves us.

A. FILL IN THE BLANKS

1. Jesus is true God because ...., and in him there is .... (38)
2. Jesus is true God from ...., begotten ...., consubstantial .... (39)
3. Jesus Christ is true man because he, the Son ...., was .... (40)
4. As man, Jesus thought with a human ...., acted with a human .... (40)

5. Jesus joined himself with every human being except in ....(40)
6. Jesus was close to people, the virtuous and ...., the poor and ...., especially .... (41)
7. In Christ's concern for people we see ....(42)

B. BIBLE READING

John 11:1-45

Lazarus Raised from the Dead

The sisters of Lazarus, Martha and Mary, sent this message to Jesus, "Lord, the one you love is ill." After learning that Lazarus was ill, Jesus remained for two more days in the place where he was.

When Martha heard that Jesus was coming, she went forth to meet him.

Jesus said to her, "Your brother will rise again."

Martha replied, "I know that he will rise again in the resurrection on the last day."

Jesus then said to her, "I am the resurrection and the life. Whoever believes in me, even though he dies, will live, and everyone who lives and believes in me will never die. Do you believe this?"

"Yes, Lord," she replied. "I believe that you are the Christ, the Son of God, the one who is to come into the world."

Mary came to the place where Jesus was, and as soon as she saw him, she fell at his feet. When Jesus saw her weeping, and beheld the Jews who were with her also weeping, he became deeply moved in spirit. He asked, "Where have you laid him?" They said to him, "Lord, come and see." Jesus began to weep.

Jesus came to the tomb. It was a cave, with a stone closing the entrance. Jesus said, "Take away the stone." Martha, the dead man's sister, said to him, "Lord, by now there will be a stench, for he has been dead for four days."

Jesus replied, "Did I not tell you that if you have faith you will see the glory of God?"

And so they removed the stone. Then Jesus looked up and said, "Father, I thank you for hearing me. I know that you always hear me, but I have said this for the sake of the people standing here, so that they may believe that it was you who sent me."

When he had said this, he cried out in a loud voice, "Lazarus, come out!" The dead man came out, his hands and feet bound with linen bands, and his face wrapped in a cloth. Then Jesus said to them, "Untie him and let him go free."

This caused many of the Jews who had come to visit Mary, and had seen what Jesus did, to believe in him.

Jesus raises Lazarus from the dead.

Discussion:

1. What did Jesus say to Martha?
2. What did Martha say to Jesus when he asked whether she believed in him?
3. How did Jesus pray to his Father?
4. How did Jesus raise Lazarus from the dead?
5. Why did this miracle prove that Jesus is true God?
6. How did this miracle show that Jesus was true man?

C. PRACTICE

1. We worship Jesus Christ even in his human nature because that human nature belongs to the Second Divine Person, the eternal Son of God. At Mass we offer Jesus, who died for us on the Cross as a sacrifice to the heavenly Father. At Holy Communion Jesus comes to us as God and man to be the food of our soul.
2. We can worship Christ in his human nature also through devotion to the Sacred Heart of Jesus. The heart of Jesus is here taken as a symbol of his manhood, the infinite love of Christ, and the mercy he has for sinners. Devotion to the Sacred Heart of Jesus in the Blessed Sacrament is one of the best means of growing in our love for him.

JESUS SPEAKS:

"The works that my Father has given me to accomplish, the very works that I am doing, testify about me, that the Father has sent me." (Jn 5:36)

"I speak of what I have seen in my Father's presence. . . . If God were your father, you would love me, for I came from God. . . . I do know him, . . . and I keep his word. . . . Amen, amen, I say to you, before Abraham was, I AM." (Jn 8:38, 42, 55, 58)

"Father, the hour has come. Glorify your Son, so that your Son may glorify you, since you have given him authority over all people, so that he may give eternal life to all those you have given him. . . . So now, Father, glorify me in your presence with the glory I had with you before the world began." (Jn 17:1-2, 5)

CHAPTER 8

Jesus Christ, Savior and Redeemer of the World

43. Why is Jesus Christ our Savior and Redeemer?

Jesus Christ is our Savior and Redeemer because as God made man he (1) preached the Gospel of the kingdom of God and (2) gave himself up to death out of love for his Father and for us.

God sent his Son to free people from the power of Satan and make peace between God and people. To do this Jesus had to become man, to preach his truth about the kingdom of his Father. He said to the people, "The time of fulfillment has arrived, and the kingdom of God is close at hand. Repent, and believe in the gospel" (Mk 1:15). Jesus continued preaching even though the religious leaders of the Jewish people were trying to harm him. They finally arranged to have him put to death by the Romans because he claimed to be the Son of God. Jesus is truly our Savior.

(2) Jesus is also our Redeemer because he paid our debt for sin and bought heaven back for us. He offered his life for the love of us and for the glory of his Father. He did his Father's will to honor him and to make people happy forever in God's kingdom. The Father now gives his own divine life of grace to people who turn to him in faith.

44. How did Christ redeem mankind?

By his Death and Resurrection, Christ redeemed mankind from slavery to sin and to the devil.

In obedience to his Father's will Jesus gave himself for us in his passion and arose from the dead that he might redeem us from sin and make us a people pleasing to the Father. He is the Messiah, God's own Son. He often said that what he was doing was done that the Scriptures might be fulfilled, because he saw his Father's will in them. We were slaves of the devil because of original sin and because of our personal sins. But Jesus made us free with the freedom of the children of God, for by his Resurrection he destroyed death and gave us the life of grace.

45. How does the risen Lord now help us?

Risen truly, the Lord (1) gives us the divine life of grace (2) and pours out his Holy Spirit upon us.

(1) By dying Jesus destroyed our death and by rising he gave back our life. He now shares with us his divine life of grace, especially through the sacraments.

(2) Jesus gives us his Holy Spirit to make us holy and pleasing to God. We must live the life of God as Jesus did. The Father gives his own life to people who turn to him in faith. The Father, Son, and Holy Spirit come and share their love with those who give themselves to Jesus. In this way Jesus makes us a new People of God.

A. FILL IN THE BLANKS

1. Jesus is our Savior and Redeemer because as .... he (1) preached .... and (2) .... (43)
2. By his .... Christ redeemed mankind from .... (44)
3. Risen truly, the Lord (1) gives us .... and (2) pours out .... (45)

B. BIBLE READING

Matthew 27:33-50
Luke 23:34-43
John 19:25-30

Jesus Dies on the Cross

When Jesus reached Calvary, he was stripped of his garments and crucified. Above his head was inscribed the charge against him: "This is Jesus, the King of the Jews." Two thieves were crucified with him, one on his right and the other on his left.

From the Cross, Jesus said, "Father, forgive them, for they do not know what they are doing." One of the thieves said to him, "Jesus, remember me when you come into your kingdom."

Jesus said to him, "Amen, I say to you, today you will be with me in Paradise."

Standing near the cross of Jesus were his mother and his mother's sister, Mary the wife of Clopas, and Mary Magdalene. When Jesus saw his mother and the disciple whom he loved standing beside her, he said to his mother, "Woman, behold, your son." Then he said to the disciple, "Behold, your mother." And from that hour the disciple took her into his home.

About three o'clock Jesus cried out in a loud voice, "My God, my God, why have you forsaken me?"

In order that the Scriptures might be fulfilled, Jesus said, "I thirst." Someone ran off, soaked a sponge with sour wine, put it on a stick, and gave it to him to drink. Then Jesus again cried out in a loud voice and gave up his spirit.

Discussion:

1. What sign did Pilate have placed on the Cross?
2. What prayer did Jesus say for those who crucified him?
3. How did Jesus pray to his Father from the Cross?
4. What did Jesus say to his mother before he died?
5. Why did Jesus die on the Cross?

C. PRACTICE

1. The best way to honor Jesus Christ, our Savior and Redeemer, is to offer the Holy Sacrifice of the Mass in union with him. The Mass is the unbloody memorial and renewal of the sacrifice of the Cross. At Mass we remember the love of Jesus who gave his life to save us, and we receive his sacrificed and risen body in Holy Communion.
2. All Catholic churches have a series of fourteen images showing the various scenes in the Passion and Death of Jesus, called "The Stations of the Cross." This devotion is one of the most highly blessed devotions in the Church, one that will give us a deeper understanding of the love and mercy of God as well as a greater sorrow for our sins.

The Father and the Son sent us the Holy Spirit

Part Four — THE HOLY SPIRIT

CHAPTER 9
The Holy Spirit in the Church and in the Life of the Christian

46. Who is the Holy Spirit?

The Holy Spirit is God, and the Third Person of the Blessed Trinity.

The Holy Spirit is the Third Person of the Blessed Trinity, truly God, just as the Father and the Son are truly God. He is the love of the Father and the Son.

47. What is the work of the Holy Spirit in the world?

The Holy Spirit carries out Christ's work when people answer God's invitation to love him and one another.

The Holy Spirit was already at work in the world before Jesus rose from the dead and ascended into heaven. But to finish the work of the salvation of all people, Jesus sent the Holy Spirit from the Father. The Spirit now carries out his work of salvation in the souls of people and spreads the Church throughout the world among those who are willing to answer God's invitation to love him and one another.

48. What did Christ say about the Holy Spirit?

Christ promised that the Spirit of Truth would (1) come and (2) remain within us.

Jesus promised to send the Holy Spirit when he said to his apostles, "I will ask the Father, and he will give you another Advocate to be with you forever, the Spirit of Truth whom the world cannot accept because it neither sees him nor knows him. But you know him, because he dwells with you and will be in you" (Jn 14:16-17).

49. When did the Holy Spirit come into the world?

The Holy Spirit came at Pentecost, never to depart.

Fifty days after Easter, on Pentecost Sunday, the Holy Spirit came to the early Church and changed the apostles from weak, fearful men to brave men of faith that Christ needed to spread his Gospel to the nations.

50. Where is the Holy Spirit present in a special way?

The Holy Spirit is present in a special way in the Church, the community of those who believe in Christ as Lord.

The Holy Spirit is present in the Catholic Church to help it to continue the work of Christ in the world. By his presence people are moved by his grace to unite themselves with God and others in sincere love and to fulfill their duties to God and others. He makes the Church pleasing to God because of the divine life of grace that he gives. By the power of the Gospel he makes the Church grow. He renews it with his gifts and leads it to perfect union with Jesus.

51. What does the Holy Spirit do for the Church?

The Holy Spirit gives his divine life of grace to the Church.

Before ascending into heaven, Jesus gave his apostles a command to teach all nations and to baptize them, and he also promised to remain with them: "Teach them to observe all that I have commanded you. And behold, I am with you always, to the end of the world" (Mt 28:20).

Jesus is with his Church also through the gift of the Holy Spirit. He promised this the night before he died. "It is better for you that I depart. For if I do not go away, the Advocate will not come to you, whereas if I go, I will send him to you" (Jn 16:7).

Through the Holy Spirit the Church is able to carry on the work of salvation given to it by Christ. The crucified and risen Jesus leads people to the Father by sending the Holy Spirit upon the People of God. The Holy Spirit came to remain with the Church forever. The Church was publicly made known to the people. The Gospel began to spread among the nations. Today the Holy Spirit is still the soul of the apostolate of the Church.

The Holy Spirit guides the Pope, bishops, and priests of the Church in their work of teaching Christ's doctrine, guiding souls, and giving God's grace to the people through the sacraments. He directs all the work of Christ in the Church—the care of the sick, the teaching of children, the guidance of youth, the comforting of the sorrowful, the support of the needy.

The Holy Spirit guides the People of God in knowing the truth. He prays in them and makes them remember that they are adopted children of God. He brings the Church together in love and worship.

52. How should we honor the Holy Spirit?

We should honor the Holy Spirit by (1) loving him as our God and (2) letting him guide us in life.

(1) We should love and honor the indwelling Spirit as our God as we honor the Father and the Son. St. Paul reminds us to do so. "Do you not realize that you are God's temple, and that the Spirit of God dwells in you?" (1 Cor 3:16).

(2) Since the Holy Spirit is always with us if we are in the state of grace, we should often ask him for the light and strength we need to live a holy life and to save our soul.

A. FILL IN THE BLANKS

1. The Holy Spirit is..........., and the .... Person of the Blessed Trinity. (46)
2. The Holy Spirit carries out ....when people answer God's invitation to .... (47)
3. Christ promised that the Spirit of Truth would (1) .... and (2) .... (48)
4. The Holy Spirit came at .... (49)
5. The Holy Spirit is present in a special way in ...., the community of those who .... (50)
6. The Holy Spirit gives ....to the Church. (51)
7. We should honor the Holy Spirit by (1) .... and (2) .... (52)

B. BIBLE READING Acts of the Apostles 2:1-43

The Descent of the Holy Spirit

After they returned to Jerusalem after the Ascension of Jesus, the apostles went to the upper room where they were staying. All of these were constantly engaged in prayer, together with the women and Mary, the Mother of Jesus, and with the brethren. Together they numbered about one hundred and twenty.

When the day of Pentecost arrived, they were all assembled together in one place. Suddenly, there came from heaven a sound similar to that of a violent wind, and it filled the entire house in which they were sitting. Then there appeared to them tongues as of fire, which separated and came to rest on each one of them. All of them were filled with the Holy Spirit and began to speak in different languages, as the Spirit enabled them to do so.

Now staying in Jerusalem there were devout Jews from every nation under heaven. *They all were astounded and perplexed.*

Peter addressed the crowd: "Men of Israel, hear these words. Jesus of Nazareth was... handed over into the hands of lawless men. Crucifying him, you killed him. However, God raised him up.... Of that we are all witnesses. Exalted at God's right hand, he received from the Father the promise of the Holy Spirit and has poured out what you now see and hear."

Pentecost

Those who accepted his message were baptized, and on that day about three thousand people were added to their number. They devoted themselves to the teaching of the apostles and to the communal fellowship, to the breaking of the bread and to prayers.

A sense of awe was felt by all for many wonders and signs were performed by the apostles.

Discussion:

1. Who were present in the upper room in prayer?
2. How did the Holy Spirit come upon the people in the upper room?
3. What did Peter say to the crowd on Pentecost?
4. How many people were converted on that day?
5. What did the apostles do after Pentecost?

C. PRACTICE

1. Since the Holy Spirit is the soul of the Church, the Mystical Body of Christ, he joins the members of the Church to one another and to Christ, their Head. Through his grace he is the cause of every good action in all parts of the Body. We should pray to him for the growth of the Church in members and in holiness.
2. Since the Holy Spirit is personally present and active in all the members of the Church, we should love him as we love the Father and the Son in the Holy Trinity. He is our friend and the loving guest of our soul through his grace. We should turn to him for help that we may live a good Christian life by loving God and our neighbor.

JESUS SPEAKS:

"I will ask the Father, and he will give you another Advocate to be with you forever, the Spirit of Truth whom the world cannot accept because it neither sees him nor knows him. But you know him, because he dwells with you and will be in you." (Jn 14:16-17)

"The Advocate, the Holy Spirit, whom the Father will send in my name, will teach you everything and remind you of all that I have said to you." (Jn 14:26)

Part Five — THE CHURCH

CHAPTER 10 The Church, People of God

53. When did the Church begin?

The Church, founded by Christ, began in his Death and Resurrection.

Through his Death and Resurrection, Jesus has earned for us the privilege of belonging to God's holy family. To enter that family we need sanctifying grace, a sharing in the life of Christ. We first receive grace when we are baptized. By the power of the Resurrection, we are inserted into the Mystical Body of Christ. We are no longer under the dominion of sin; with him we are heirs of heaven; we, like him, shall rise from the dead.

The Church officially began when the Holy Spirit entered into the followers of Jesus on the day of Pentecost. The apostles announced to everybody the good news of what Jesus had done and invited their hearers to believe in him and live by his Spirit.

54. What is the Church?

The Church is the new People of God, prepared for in the Old Testament, and given life, growth, and direction by Christ in the Holy Spirit. It is the work of God's saving love in Christ.

Through Israel, the first People of God, God kept his promise to send the world a Savior who would gather all people into God's family. Jesus, God's own Son, born of Mary, was a descendant of David. He brought peace to his people and freed their souls from sin. He is our Savior. Jesus sent his Spirit and life upon his followers as he promised. To proclaim the Good News of salvation to all people everywhere in all times, Jesus formed into one body his followers, the community of believers, the new People of God. He called this body his Church.

55. What are the gifts of God in the Catholic Church?

The gifts of God in the Catholic Church are (1) the truths of faith, (2) the sacraments, and (3) the ministries inherited from the apostles.

(1) To carry on Christ's teaching the apostles were given the power and duty to teach his doctrine to the world. They were appointed by him to be our shepherds or spiritual leaders so that through them and their successors he would guide us to the kingdom of heaven. Jesus said, "Whoever listens to you listens to me, and whoever rejects you rejects me. And whoever rejects me rejects the one who sent me" (Lk 10:16).

(2) Christ taught the apostles that his grace was to be given to others through them. Through them he would forgive sin, give his Body and Blood to the world, and teach people in his name. Through the apostles and their successors, to whom these powers were entrusted, the Church administers the sacraments for the salvation of God's People.

(3) With the powers given them by Christ, the apostles were to be his witnesses in the world. He said to them before ascend-

ing into heaven, "You will receive power when the Holy Spirit comes upon you, and then you will be my witnesses not only in Jerusalem, but throughout Judea and Samaria, and indeed to the farthest ends of the earth" (Acts 1:8). Jesus continued, through his apostles and their successors, to be king, priest, and teacher to his people.

56. What does the Church do for mankind through these gifts?

Through these gifts of God, the Church is able to act and grow as a community in Christ, serving mankind and giving people his saving word and activity.

(1) Through God's truth, the sacraments, and the ministry of the priesthood, the Church is able to grow. Peter was Christ's chief ambassador on earth. The whole Church was entrusted to his care. The apostles share their responsibility with others, called bishops.

(2) Today the Church continues, through bishops, aided by priests, to be a community in Christ and to serve mankind by giving people Christ's saving truth and his divine life through grace and the sacraments.

57. Why is the Church missionary?

The Church is missionary because every member of the Church shares the command from Christ to carry the Good News of Christ's teaching to all mankind by word and example.

The Church gives Christian witness as a community of believers and brotherly love by the preaching of the Gospel and by its service to others. Jesus said to his apostles, "All authority in heaven and on earth has been given to me. Go, therefore, and make disciples of all nations, baptizing them in the name of the Father and of the Son and of the Holy Spirit, and teaching them to observe all that I have commanded you. And behold, I am with you always, to the end of the world" (Mt 28:18-20).

58. Why is the Church a society with leaders?

In God's plan, the Church is a society with leaders, that is, with a hierarchy. It is a people guided by its bishops, who are in union with the Pope.

Through ordination of bishops and priests, the powers of Jesus Christ have been handed down in the Catholic Church for more than 2,000 years. Bishops and priests are those in Christ's Mystical Body who have the authority to teach for Christ, to shepherd his flock, and to dispense his graces to the world. Christ lives and works through his bishops and priests in his Church.

59. Who is the Pope?

The Pope, the Bishop of Rome, is (1) the Vicar of Christ, who has succeeded to the office of Peter in his care and guidance of the whole flock of Christ and (2) the head of the college of bishops.

(1) The Pope, the Bishop of Rome, is the successor of St. Peter, being supreme shepherd of the Church of Christ, having all the rights, powers, and duties of Peter.

(2) Jesus solemnly told Peter he was to be supreme shepherd, the head of the Church. "And I say to you: You are Peter, and on this rock I will build my Church, and the gates of the netherworld will not prevail against it. I will give you the keys of the kingdom of heaven. Whatever you bind on earth shall be bound in heaven, and whatever you loose on earth shall be loosed in heaven" (Mt 16:18-19).

(3) While the Pope is the successor of St. Peter, the Catholic bishops are the successors of the other apostles. Christ made the apostles as a stable group or college. They were jointly responsible for spreading the Gospel of Christ to the whole world. Jesus

said to Peter, "I have prayed that your own faith may not fail. And once you have turned back, you must strengthen your brethren" (Lk 22:32). When the Church, that is, the college of bishops in communion with the Pope, teaches solemnly in the name of God, the teaching is infallible, that is, it cannot be mistaken in matters of faith or morals.

60. What is the role of the Pope and bishops in the Church?

The role of the Pope and the bishops is to teach, sanctify, and govern the Church.

Christ conferred on the apostles and their successors the duty of teaching, sanctifying, and governing in his name and power. When a third time Jesus asked Peter, "Simon, son of John, do you love me?" Peter was hurt that Jesus had asked a third time, "Do you love me?" "Lord," he said to him, "you know everything. You know that I love you." Jesus said to him, "Feed my sheep" (Jn 21:17).

61. What do the faithful owe the Pope and bishops?

The faithful, the community of faith, owe the Pope and bishops respect and obedience.

We serve God and his Church by obeying the Fourth Commandment of God in honoring, loving, respecting, and obeying the Pope as successor of St. Peter, our bishop who is our shepherd, and our priests ordained for the loving service of the faithful.

62. What is the work of the Holy Spirit in the Church?

The work of the Holy Spirit is to (1) preserve the Church as the Body of Christ and his bride so that it may be faithful to him in holiness till the end of the world and (2) help the Church always to purify and renew itself and its members.

(1) The Holy Spirit brings about a union between Christ and his members. St. Paul describes this union as the Body of Christ. Christ himself is head of that Body, while those who belong to him are its members. They are united closely with the head and with each other by a strong interior bond, which is the Holy Spirit.

The Church is also called the Bride of Christ. St. Paul says that Jesus loved his bride, the Church. He made her beautiful and gave his life for her.

(2) With the help of the grace of the Holy Spirit, the Church is constantly purified and renewed spiritually. Without these helps of actual grace, it is impossible to do anything toward our own salvation or the salvation of others. These graces help us to live well as God's children and followers of Jesus Christ.

A. FILL IN THE BLANKS

1. The Church, founded by ....began in ....(53)
2. The Church is ...., prepared for in ...., and given life, growth, and direction by .... in the .... It is the work of .... (54)
3. The gifts of God in the Catholic Church are (1) the ...., (2) the ...., and (3) the ....inherited from .... (55)
4. Through these gifts of God, the Church is able to ...., ... and giving people ....(56)
5. The Church is missionary because every member of the Church shares the command from Christ to .... by word and example. (57)
6. In God's plan, the Church is ...., that is, with.................... It is a people guided by ...., who are in union with .... (58)
7. The Pope, the Bishop of Rome, is (1) ...., who has succeeded to the office of ....in his care and guidance of the whole flock of Christ and (2) .... (59)
8. The role of the Pope and the bishops is to ...., ..., and .... the Church. (60)

9. The faithful, the community of ...., owe the Pope and bishops .... (61)
10. The work of the Holy Spirit is to (1) ....so that it may be faithful to him in ....till the end of the world and (2) .... the Church always to .... and .... itself and its members. (62)

B. BIBLE READING

Matthew 16:13-19

Peter, the Head of the Church

When Jesus came to the region of Caesarea Philippi, he asked his disciples, "Who do people say that the Son of Man is?"

They replied, "Some say John the Baptist; others, Elijah; and still others, Jeremiah or one of the Prophets."

"But you," he said to them, "who do you say that I am?"

Simon Peter replied, "You are the Christ, the Son of the living God."

Then Jesus said to him in reply, "Blessed are you, Simon son of Jonah. For flesh and blood has not revealed this to you but my heavenly Father. And I say to you: You are Peter, and on this rock I will build my Church, and the gates of the netherworld will not prevail

against it. I will give you the keys of the kingdom of heaven. Whatever you bind on earth shall be bound in heaven, and whatever you loose on earth shall be loosed in heaven."

By these words Jesus promised to make Peter the head of his Church. Keys are a symbol of power. Jesus meant that Peter was to have power to govern his Church.

Discussion:

1. Who did people think Jesus was?
2. Who did Peter say Jesus was?
3. Why did Jesus say Peter was blessed?
4. What did Jesus say to Peter about his Church?
5. What did these words of Jesus to Peter mean?
6. Who is the successor of Peter today?

C. PRACTICE

1. Catholic laypeople have a part in the mission of the Church. By the very fact of their membership in the Mystical Body of Christ they have a share in the apostolate of the Church. Part of the Church's task is to form the conscience of the individual Christian in order that he might bring the principles of Christ into education, marriage, recreation, business, politics, etc. The Catholic layperson must be a witness to Christ in the world and by prayer and good example share in the missionary apostolate of the Church.

2. In making Peter the supreme pastor of his flock, Christ gave him the gift of infallibility in matters of faith and morals. "The *Pope*, Bishop of Rome and Peter's successor 'is the perpetual and visible source and foundation of the unity both of the bishops and of the whole company of the faithful.' 'For the Roman Pontiff, by reason of his office as Vicar of Christ, and as pastor of the entire Church has full, supreme, and universal power over the whole Church, a power which he can always exercise unhindered' " (CCC 882). This teaching is affirmed in Vatican II documents and in the *Code of Canon Law*.

CHAPTER

11 The Church as Community

63. Why is the Church a community?

The Church is a community because it shares together the life of Christ; it is a people assembled by God.

The Church is the worldwide community of those whom God has called to give witness to his Son Jesus and to the new life he has brought to us. As members of this community, we are joined to Christ through Baptism; we share his divine life through grace which reaches us especially through the sacraments.

64. Are all persons equal in the Church?

All persons in the Church are united and equal as the one People of God.

All members in the Church are united and equal, but they have different responsibilities. Just as God made Moses the leader of his people in the Old Testament, so Christ gave to his apostles and their successors the right to teach and to command in his name. These powers are given for the service and welfare of the whole People of God. Living in the world, the laity are called to work for the sanctification of the world by carrying out their tasks according to the spirit of the Gospel.

65. Who has a vocation to holiness in the Church?

In the Church every individual has a call from God, a vocation to holiness.

With Christ we have already died to sin and risen to newness of life. He pours into our souls that very life of divine sonship that filled him in his own Resurrection. This he does through the sacraments of the Church he founded. In the Church Jesus wishes to continue his own life in us for the glory of the Father. This Christ-life within us is the holiness to which God has called every person in the Church. This is a life of love and obedience to the Father.

66. Why does each member of the Church deserve respect?

Each member of the Church deserves respect, since all join in the one cause of Christ.

Dedication to Christ means obeying the commandments, fulfilling the duties of our state of life, accepting the suffering God permits in our life, striving to do all for the love of God, and working to spread the reign of Christ. Everyone in the Church who in this way joins in the one cause of Christ deserves our deepest respect. Besides, through Baptism we are united in the Body of Christ of which he is the head.

67. Who directs the work in the cause of Christ in the Church?

The Pope and the bishops direct the work in the cause of Christ in the Church, in every rite, diocese, parish, and mission.

The Pope is a visible sign of Jesus and the symbol of unity for the Church. Together with the bishops, and as their head, he teaches and governs the universal Church. The bishops are visible signs of Jesus in each locality and the symbol of unity for the

Church there. Each diocesan bishop is responsible for teaching and governing the Church in that locality. Throughout the world, all bishops, together with the Pope, are the official witnesses to the faith of the whole Church and have the responsibility for its life, aided by priests.

68. Is Christ present in each diocese, parish, and mission?

In each diocese, parish, and mission, Christ is present, and by his power the one, holy, catholic, and apostolic Church is gathered together.

Through the grace of the Sacraments of Baptism and the Holy Eucharist, Christ is present in us. The Christ-life within us means that we open our minds to him by faith so that we have the same outlook that he had. We open our hearts to him that he may live in us his own life of love and dedication to the Father. By this power the Catholic Church is gathered together even in the smallest parish.

A. FILL IN THE BLANKS

1. The Church is a community because ....; it is............................... assembled by God. (63)
2. All persons in the Church are united and equal as ....(64)
3. In the Church every individual has a call from God, a vocation to .... (65)
4. Each member of the Church deserves respect, since ....(66)
5. The Pope and the bishops direct the work in the cause of Christ in the Church, ... (67)
6. In each ...., ..., and ...., Christ is present, and by his power the one, holy, catholic, and apostolic Church is .... (68)

B. BIBLE READING

Matthew 5:1-16

The Sermon on the Mount

Seeing the great crowd of people following him, Jesus went up on the mountain and sat down where the people could gather around him. He taught them with these words:

"Blessed are the poor in spirit, for theirs is the kingdom of heaven. Blessed are those who mourn, for they will be comforted. Blessed are the meek, for they will inherit the earth.

"Blessed are those who hunger and thirst for justice, for they will have their fill.

"Blessed are the merciful, for they will obtain mercy.

"Blessed are the pure of heart, for they will see God. Blessed are the peacemakers, for they will be called children of God. Blessed are those who are persecuted in the cause of justice, for theirs is the kingdom of heaven."

"Blessed are you when people insult you and persecute you and utter all kinds of calumnies against you for my sake. Rejoice and be glad, for your reward will be great in heaven."

You have the blessing of Jesus when you try to do right, although your companions may make fun of you and try to stop you. When people sneer at you and say bad things about you because you try to do the right thing, do not be discouraged. Be glad, for you will have a great reward in heaven.

Jesus also said,"You are the salt of the earth. But if salt loses its taste, what can be done to make it salty once again? It is no longer good for anything, and thus it is cast out and trampled underfoot.

"You are the light of the world. A city built upon a mountain cannot be hidden. Nor would someone light a lamp and then put it under a basket; rather, it is placed upon a lampstand so that it may afford light to all in the house. In the same way, your light must shine so that it can be seen by others; this will enable them to observe your good works and give praise to your Father in heaven."

When we love Jesus we are like the salt of the earth. As salt preserves things from rotting, we can keep the world from evil by our good example. We are the salt of the earth in the measure that we are holy.

As Jesus is the light of the world by his holy doctrine and example, so too we may be the light of the world by the brightness of our good example. By the light of our holy life, we can scatter the darkness of the spirit of the world.

Discussion:

1. What did Jesus say about those who are poor in spirit? About those who mourn? About the meek?
2. What did Jesus say about those who hunger and thirst for justice? About those who are merciful?
3. What did Jesus say about the pure of heart? About the peacemakers? About those persecuted in the cause of justice?
4. Why did Jesus say we should be the salt of the earth?
5. Why did Jesus say we should be the light of the world?
6. How can we see from Christ's words that everyone in the Church is called to holiness?

C. PRACTICE

1. Through Jesus Christ we have been made members of the family of God. We are joined to Christ and one another in a union that is far closer than any union on earth. Our Lord himself compared it to the marvelous union of the Blessed Trinity. Because we belong to the family of God, we are a community; we are never alone. We are one with Christ and one with one another in the union of the Mystical Body of Christ here on earth. So close is this union that whatever we do or fail to do to one another, we do or fail to do to Christ himself. The things that separate us from one another—wealth, social position, color of skin, difference in nationality—are all small compared to the bond that unites us as members of Christ and one another. We must ever keep in mind the important fact that whatever we do to anyone, we do to Christ. We should make an effort to see Christ in our neighbor.

2. The center of the parish and the source of its life is Christ. He is truly present in the Eucharist. He is also present in the people who have the divine life of grace, but not in the sacramental way as in the Holy Eucharist. Christ is present, too, among the community of Christians who meet with him in their midst. Through their meeting with one another in a spirit of mutual love, the people of the parish are a witness of Christ's presence among them. They are the sign by which the world can know them as members of Christ's kingdom.

JESUS SPEAKS:

"Deal with others as you would like them to deal with you. This is the Law and the Prophets." (Mt 7:12)

"You did not choose me. Rather, I chose you. And I appointed you to go out and bear fruit, fruit that will remain, so that the Father may give you whatever you ask him in my name." (Jn 15:16)

CHAPTER

12 The Quest for Unity

69. Why is Christian unity in faith and love God's will?

Christian unity in faith and love is God's will because Christ willed that all who believe in him be one, so that the world might know that he was sent by the Father.

There is but one Church. Jesus brought the same good news to all and called all to the same new life. His Church is the union of those who follow his call. The Roman Catholic Church is the worldwide community of the followers of Jesus that is united around the Pope. The night before he died Jesus prayed for Christian unity. "I pray . . . also for those who through their word will come to believe in me. May they all be one. As you, Father, are in me and I in you, may they also be in us so that the world may believe that you have sent me" (Jn 17:20-21).

70. How should Catholics promote Christian unity?

Catholics should promote Christian unity by (1) being deeply concerned over the sad divisions of Christians, (2) taking the first steps in meeting with non-Catholics, and (3) trying to make the Church more faithful to Christ and to what she received from the apostles.

(1) Christians are not one because historical differences and bitterness have driven the followers of Jesus apart. Men's understanding of Jesus and the meaning of his life and teaching also differs.

(2) Prayer and work for Christian unity are important to Catholic life. Catholics should take the first steps in meeting with non-Catholics.

(3) Catholics should help to fulfill the Church's mission in our time. They should carry out the Gospel of Christ in their own life and dedicate themselves to extend his message to others.

71. What do we believe concerning the Catholic Church?

We believe that the Catholic Church is the ordinary means of salvation and should desire to share her fullness with all.

We believe that Jesus Christ entrusted his work of redemption to his Church. He said to his first disciples, "As the Father has sent me, so I send you" (Jn 20:21). Not to the individual, but to the Church was the promise made by Christ: "I will ask the Father, and he will give you another Advocate to be with you forever" (Jn 14:16).

We believe that only through the Church can we know with certainty what God wills us to believe and to do in order to reach salvation. Only through the Church can we find the security and certainty about the meaning of our human lives.

We believe the Catholic Church has the ordinary means of salvation. She has God's truth, and the sacraments, which are the channels of God's grace.

72. Why should Catholics show respect for all people of goodwill?

A unity of all people under God should be a concern of Catholics because God has given to everyone dignity, freedom, and eternal importance.

Man, because he has a spiritual soul, has dominion over the other earthly creatures and is a more perfect image of God than anything else on this earth. Man is made for God. He has a special dignity and value as a human being. He is free and he will live forever. This makes him deserving of our respect.

As Christ sent his apostles to teach and to be witnesses to him in the world, so, too, he wants us to share in this mission. The duty of proclaiming the Gospel and making its power felt in the lives of others belongs not only to bishops and priests but also to the laity in the Church. Every Catholic man and woman is called by God to be an apostle, a messenger of Christ to the world. Therefore the unity of all people under God should be our concern so that our Lord's prayer for unity may be fulfilled.

A. FILL IN THE BLANKS

1. Christian unity in faith and love is God's will because ...., so that the world might know that .... (69)
2. Catholics should promote Christian unity by (1) being ...., (2) taking the first steps in ...., and (3) trying to make the Church more faithful to and to .... (70)
3. We believe that the Catholic Church is .... and should desire to .... (71)
4. A unity of all people under God should be a concern of Catholics because .... (72)

B. BIBLE READING John 10:11-18

The Good Shepherd

When Jesus was speaking to the crowds, he said, "I am the good shepherd. The good shepherd lays down his life for the sheep. The hired hand, who is not the shepherd nor the owner of the sheep, sees the wolf approaching, and he leaves the sheep and runs away, while the wolf catches and scatters them. He runs away because he is only a hired hand and he has no concern for the sheep.

"I am the good shepherd. I know my own, and my own know me, just as the Father knows me and I know the Father. And I lay down my life for the sheep.

"I have other sheep too that do not belong to this fold. I must lead them as well, and they will hear my voice. Thus, there will only be one flock, one shepherd.

"This is why the Father loves me, because I lay down my life in order to take it up again. No one takes it away from me. I lay it down of my own free will. And as I have the power to lay it down, I have the power to take it up again. This command I have received from my Father."

Discussion:

1. What does the good shepherd do for his sheep?
2. What does the hired hand do when the wolf approaches?
3. How does Jesus know his sheep?
4. What does Jesus do for his sheep?
5. What does Jesus say about the other sheep that do not belong to his fold?
6. How does the story of the good shepherd show the need for Christian unity?

C. PRACTICE

1. Jesus Christ took to himself one Mystical Body. That Body is the Catholic Church. In the course of history, disputes, misunderstandings, the pride and greed of men, and weaknesses and abuses within the Church itself have resulted in harm to the Body of Christ. Millions have been separated from the unity of the Body. Many good people today are deprived, through no fault of their own, of the life-giving sacraments and of sharing in Christ's sacrifice. Christ wants all of them to be reunited to his Mystical Body, the Catholic Church. Even though these people are not aware that the Church is the one true Church of Christ, it is through the Church that they receive their divine life and their salvation. Hence the Church urges Catholics to promote Christian unity by understanding and concern for separated Christians, by taking the first steps in meeting with them, by being a good example for them, and by praying for the unity that Jesus desired as he prayed to his heavenly Father.
2. In its Decree on Ecumenism (*Unitatis Redintegratio*), the Second Vatican Council states: "In certain special circumstances, such as the prescribed prayers 'for unity,' and during ecumenical gatherings, it is allowable, indeed desirable that Catholics should join in prayer with their separated brethren. While "they are a true expression of the ties which still bind Catholics to their separated brethren....worship in common (*communicatio in sacris*) is not to be considered as a means to be used indiscriminately for the restoration of Christian unity" (*UR* 8). "This holy objective—the reconciliation of all Christians in the unity of the one and only Church of Christ—transcends human powers and gifts." That is why we place all our hope "in the prayer of Christ for the Church, in the love of the Father for us, and in the power of the Holy Spirit" (CCC 822). You can join Jesus in his prayer for the Church in a specific way during the Week of Prayer for Christian Unity that takes place every January.

JESUS SPEAKS:

"I pray not only on behalf of these, but also for those who through their word will come to believe in me. May they all be one. As you, Father, are in me and I in you, may they also be in us so that the world may believe that you have sent me."

(Jn 17:20-21)

CHAPTER 13 The Church as Institution for Salvation

73. Why is the Church an institution for salvation?

The Church is an institution for salvation because she is a community of the People of God with Christ as leader and head, who has given it the mission of bringing the message of salvation to all.

Through Jesus Christ we have been made members of the family of God, the People of God. We are one with Christ and one with one another in the union of the Mystical Body of Christ here on earth. So close is this union that whatever we do or fail to do to one another we do or fail to do to Christ himself.

The Church speaks the good news of God's actions in the world. It does this through her teaching and preaching, through her life and worship, through her Bible and the writings of her prophets. The mission of the Church is to bring the message of salvation to all. The Church must live the life of Jesus in his Spirit and show his love by her life of respect for and service to others.

74. What is the role of the Church in the world?

The Church is not of this world, but she speaks and listens to the world as well as tries to be seen by the world as faithful to the Gospel and as journeying toward heaven.

To his Church Christ gave the command to spread the message of salvation to all parts of the earth. God revealed his plan to save mankind and to give each of us a share in his divine life through Jesus Christ his Son. Therefore the Church both speaks and listens to the world without accepting the spirit of the world.

The Church ministers to the spiritual needs of her people by providing a community of faith, where they can find help and guidance in seeking God. The sacraments are special actions in the Church through which the life of God is given to his people.

The Church also ministers to the bodily needs of people by helping those in need, by overcoming the causes of suffering, and by building up a better life for them. But the Church always has heaven in view and continues to be a light to lead people to eternal life with God.

A. FILL IN THE BLANKS

1. The Church is an institution for salvation because ...., who has given it the mission of ....(73)
2. The Church is not of this world, but she .... as well as tries to be seen by the world as .... and as .... (74)

B. BIBLE READING

John 21:15-23

The Primacy Given to Peter

When they had finished breakfast, Jesus said to Simon Peter, "Simon, son of John, do you love me more than these?" He replied, "Yes, Lord, you know that I love you." Jesus said to him, "Feed my lambs."

Jesus said to him again, "Simon, son of John, do you love me?" He replied, "Yes, Lord, you know that I love you." Jesus said to him, "Tend my sheep."

Jesus said to him a third time, "Simon, son of John, do you love me?" Peter was hurt that Jesus had asked him a third time, "Do you love me?" "Lord," he said to him, "you know everything. You know that I love you." Jesus said to him, "Feed my sheep."

Jesus did know that Peter loved him. But he wanted to remind him that he had a work for Peter to do, a work that would demand the sacrifice of his life.

"Amen, amen, I say to you, when you were young you used to fasten your own belt and you would go wherever you wished. But when you grow old, you will stretch out your hands, and someone else will put a belt around you and take you where you do not wish to go."

He said this to indicate the kind of death by which Peter would glorify God. After this, he said to him, "Follow me."

Peter looked around and saw the disciple whom Jesus loved following them.... When Peter saw him, he said to Jesus, "Lord, what about him?" Jesus replied, "If it should be my will that he remain until I come, how does that concern you? Follow me!"

Till now Peter had only received the promise of the primacy, but after this morning meal Jesus conferred the primacy upon him in all fullness and majesty in the presence of the other apostles. It was truly divine power—divine in its origin and nature, for it represents Jesus: "Feed my lambs"; divine in its extent, for it embraces the whole Church—the hearing as well as the teaching body—and includes the entire and supreme power; divine in its operation and significance, for the whole Church—its being, attributes, stability, life, growth, and work—stands and falls with the primacy. Always the Church will feed the sheep and lambs, without distinction and without exception, on holy doctrine.

When Jesus was about to leave his sheep, he appointed Peter the shepherd in his place. As a shepherd, Peter would have his chance to lay down his life. As a youth he had been his own master; but in his old age, his hands would be stretched on a cross. Peter was crucified on Vatican Hill in Rome in the year 64.

Discussion:

1. What did Jesus ask Peter?
2. What did Jesus ask Peter to do as a proof of his love?
3. How did Jesus describe Peter's death?
4. What did Jesus have to say about John?
5. What kind of power did Jesus bestow on Peter?
6. When and where did Peter die?

C. PRACTICE

1. The people who belong to a parish are members of Christ's kingdom. Their duty is to work with the pastor in the whole life of the parish. They are to take an active part in the worship, belong to and work together in various parish organizations, support the parish financially, and carry the teaching and sanctifying action of the Church into the community in which they live and work. Since the parish is Christ in the community, its duty is to care for the members of the parish and to go out in search of those who have strayed from the practice of their faith, and of those who do not yet share the fullness of the Mystical Body of Christ.
2. It is the duty of Catholics to be mission minded. All people are meant to be incorporated into the Body of Christ, the Church,

because he died for all. Catholics can help the foreign and home missions not only by their generous contributions but also by their prayers and their zeal in promoting interest in the work of the missions.

JESUS SPEAKS:

"Amen, I say to you, whatever you did for one of the least of these brethren of mine, you did for me." (Mt 25:40)

"Whoever receives one such child in my name receives me; and whoever receives me receives not me but the one who sent me." (Mk 9:37)

"Whoever gives you a cup of water to drink because you bear the name of Christ will certainly not go unrewarded." (Mk 9:41)

"Whoever wishes to be great among you must be your servant, and whoever wishes to be first among you must be your servant." (Mt 20:26-27)

"All authority in heaven and on earth has been given to me. Go, therefore, and make disciples of all nations, baptizing them in the name of the Father and of the Son and of the Holy Spirit, and teaching them to observe all that I have commanded you. And behold, I am with you always, to the end of the world." (Mt 28:18-20)

Part Six — THE SACRAMENTS

CHAPTER 14 The Sacraments, Actions of Christ in the Church

75. How is the saving work of Christ continued in the Church?

Through the gift of the Holy Spirit, the Church (1) enjoys the presence of Christ and (2) carries on his ministry and saving mission.

(1) Before ascending into heaven, Jesus gave his apostles a command to teach all nations and to baptize them. He promised to be with them. "Teach them to observe all that I have commanded you. And behold, I am with you always, to the end of the world" (Mt 28:20).

Jesus is with his Church also through the gift of the Holy Spirit. He promised this the night before he died. "For if I do not go away, the Advocate will not come to you, whereas if I go, I will send him to you" (Jn 16:7).

(2) Through the Holy Spirit the Church is able to carry on the work of salvation given to her by Christ.

76. What means does the Church have for carrying on Christ's work?

The Church has been given special means for carrying on Christ's work, namely, the sacraments which he instituted.

Christ's work of salvation is continued in the Church especially in the sacraments. The sacraments are special actions in the Church through which the life of God is given to his people.

77. What do the sacraments do?

"Celebrated worthily in faith, the sacraments confer the grace that they signify. They are *efficacious* because in them Christ himself is at work."

The sacraments are signs that we can see, which let us know that God's grace is being given to the soul of the person who receives the sacrament. We can see the signs with our bodily eyes, but it is only through faith that we know God's grace is given to us. We believe this on the word of Jesus himself who gave us the sacraments to make it possible for us to share God's own life, through grace. This grace helps us to worship God and to love God and our neighbor.

In the sacraments the words together with the action make up the sacred sign. Water, since it is so necessary for life, can be used as a sign of life—a sign also of divine life in Baptism. Oil is used to strengthen and heal the body. It is used in Confirmation to show the strength we receive from this sacrament and to give us that strength. Baptism not only signifies life, it truly produces it. Confirmation not only signifies strength but gives it. Anointing of the Sick not only is a sign of health but also gives it to the soul and body.

78. What do the sacraments show?

The sacraments show that (1) God wants to make us holy and (2) we want to receive this holiness. In this way the sacraments bring us God's grace.

(1) The sacraments are the signs that Christ began, which show us that grace is being given and that they themselves produce this grace. God gave us the sacraments in order to show that he wants us to be made holy by giving us his grace. By grace we share in the very life of God himself, for through Baptism we are born again. God lives in us as in a temple. We are truly children of God through grace. All this happens when Jesus comes to us in the sacraments.

(2) We show that we are willing to receive Christ's grace if we often and earnestly receive the sacraments.

79. Why are the sacraments called actions of Christ?

Sacraments are called actions of Christ because (1) through them he gives his Spirit to Christians and makes them a holy people and (2) from Christ they get their power to make us holy.

(1) In the sacraments Christ gives us his grace, bought for us on the Cross, to help us to become more like him. The Church is the community of those whom God has called to give witness to his Son Jesus and to the new life he has brought to us. In this community of the People of God the Holy Spirit gives and strengthens the life of God through the sacraments, prayers, and works of service for others.

(2) The Church has the power of administering the sacraments, but the Church receives this power from Christ. It is Christ who baptizes, who forgives sins. It is not so much the priest who celebrates the Eucharist as Christ himself, for he offers himself in the Sacrifice of the Mass by the ministry of the priests. The action of the sacrament is the action of Christ. The priests who administer the sacraments are only ordained representatives of Christ, our high priest, and his instruments.

80. What is the purpose of the sacraments?

The purpose of the sacraments is to (1) make people holy, (2) build up the Body of Christ, the Church, and (3) give worship to God.

(1) The sacraments are the ordinary channels of God's grace and are necessary to keep the life of grace in our soul. Jesus gives us his grace to make us holy.

(2) Each of the sacraments plays an important part in the life of the Church. They give us the grace we need to become living members of the Body of Christ, which is the Church. Thus the Body of Christ grows.

(3) By means of the Eucharist Christ reoffers himself to the Father through the ministry of his priest in the Sacrifice of the Mass. This is the greatest act of worship that can be given to God. At Mass Jesus and the faithful daily adore the Father. With him they give glory to God and praise him for his mercy and generosity toward us. This we do in a manner worthy of God.

81. The Church urges Catholics to receive the sacraments in what manner?

The Church urges Catholics to receive the sacraments (1) often and with great eagerness because the sacraments were instituted to nourish Christian life and (2) with faith because they are sacraments of faith.

(1) Christ made the sacraments instruments to produce grace in us. In order that the faithful may nourish their Christian life, the Church urges all Catholics not only to understand the meaning of all the sacraments but also to receive them eagerly and frequently. (2) The more faith and love we have when we receive the sacraments, the more grace they will give us. We must not neglect to use the means God has given us to grow holy and pleasing to him by sharing his divine life.

82. What are the effects of the sacraments?

The sacraments are (1) sources of grace for individuals and communities and (2) remedies for sin and the effects of sin.

(1) Jesus Christ is the source of divine life. He gives us this life and increases it within us by means of the seven channels of grace called the sacraments. Through the sacraments Christ is with us throughout our lives to provide us with all the help and strength we need to grow in the divine life. He is always there to forgive us, to nourish us, and to prepare us for the vocation by which we serve him in the Church.

A sacrament is a sacred sign instituted by Christ to give grace. This grace is given for the benefit of the person who receives the sacrament and also for the benefit of the whole community of believers. The sacraments are instruments of divine life for the family of God.

(2) Mortal sin is the greatest evil in the world because when we choose to sin mortally, we effectively drive out of our soul the divine life of sanctifying grace and turn away from God, the source of all life, peace, and joy. But our Lord protects our soul from serious sin by giving us more sanctifying grace in the sacraments, especially in the Holy Eucharist. In addition each sacrament gives its own particular actual or sacramental graces and a right to future actual graces. These sacramental graces give us the light to see what is evil and the strength we need to fight against it. In this way our soul is strengthened against temptation. This is especially true of Holy Communion, which is a remedy for our spiritual sickness and weakness.

A. FILL IN THE BLANKS

1. Through the gift of the Holy Spirit, the Church (1) enjoys .... and (2) carries on .... (75)
2. The Church's special means for carrying on Christ's work are .... (76)

3. "Celebrated worthily in faith, ... They are *efficacious* because in them ...."(77)
4. The sacraments show that (1) God wants .... and (2) we want .... (78)
5. Sacraments are called actions of Christ because (1)..................... .... and (2) .... (79)
6. The purpose of the sacraments is to (1) ...., (2) .... and (3) ...., (80)
7. The Church urges Catholics to receive the sacraments often and with great eagerness because ....(81)
8. The Church urges Catholics to receive the sacraments with faith because ....(81)
9. The sacraments are sources of grace for..................................(82)
10. The sacraments are remedies for ....(82)

B. BIBLE READING

John 4:6-42

The Samaritan Woman

Jesus, tired from his journey, sat down at [Jacob's] well. It was about noon.

When a Samaritan woman came to draw water, Jesus said to her, "Give me some water to drink." His disciples had gone into the town to purchase food. The Samaritan woman said to him, "You are a Jew. How can you ask me, a Samaritan woman, for some water to drink?" (Jews do not share anything in common with Samaritans.)

Jesus replied, "If you recognized the gift of God and who it is that is asking you for something to drink, you would have asked him and he would have given you living water."

"Sir," the woman said, "you do not have a bucket, and the well is deep. Where can you get this living water? Are you greater than our ancestor Jacob who gave us this well and drank from it himself along with his sons and his cattle?"

Jesus said to her, "Everyone who drinks this water will be thirsty again. But whoever drinks the water that I will give him will never be thirsty. The water that I will give him will become a spring of water within him welling up to eternal life."

The woman said to him, "Sir, give me this water so that I may not be thirsty and have to come here to draw water."

When Jesus told her to call her husband, the woman responded that she had no husband. Jesus knew that she had had five husbands and that the man she was with was not her husband, and he confirmed her truth.

The woman said to him, "Sir, I can see that you are a prophet." [She later continued,] "I know that the Messiah is coming, the one who is called Christ. When he comes, he will reveal everything to us."

Jesus said to her, "I am he, the one who is speaking to you."

At this point, his disciples returned, and they were astonished to find him speaking with a woman.

The woman left behind her water jar and went off to the town, where she said to the people, "Come and see a man who told me everything I have ever done. Could this be the Christ?" And so they departed from the town and made their way to see him.

Jesus said, "I am he [Christ]."

When the Samaritans came to him, they pleaded with him to stay with them, and he remained there for two days. And many more began to believe in him because of the words he spoke to them. They said to the woman, "We have heard him for ourselves, and we are convinced that this man is truly the Savior of the world."

Discussion:

1. What was strange about Jesus' encounter with the woman at the well?
2. What did Jesus say about the living water he gives those who come to him?
3. What did Jesus answer to the woman when she mentioned the Messiah?
4. How did the woman get the people to come to Jesus?
5. What did the people say about Jesus after he stayed with them two days?
6. How does Jesus give us this "living water" through the sacraments?

C. PRACTICE

1. The more faith and love we have when we receive the sacraments, the more grace they will give us. It is true that the sacraments worthily received always give grace, even if they are received without enough preparation. But it is also true that the better prepared we are to receive them, the more grace we will receive. We should, therefore, receive the sacraments with great devotion.
2. The Sacrament of Holy Eucharist and the Sacrament of Penance are the sacraments we can receive most frequently. We should try to receive the Eucharist every Sunday or Saturday evening, and even as often as we can during the week. It would be good to receive the Sacrament of Penance at least each month in order to obtain the graces we need to lead a good Christian life.

JESUS SPEAKS:

"Abide in me, as I abide in you. Just as a branch cannot bear fruit by itself unless it abides in the vine, so you cannot bear fruit unless you abide in me." (Jn 15:4)

"I am the vine, you are the branches. Whoever abides in me, and I in him, will bear much fruit. Apart from me you can do nothing." (Jn 15:5)

CHAPTER

15 Instruction on the Sacraments

83. What is Baptism?

Baptism is the sacrament of (1) rebirth as a child of God made holy by the Spirit, (2) unity with Jesus in his Death and Resurrection, (3) cleansing from original and personal sins, and (4) welcome into the community of the Church.

(1) Baptism is a new birth as a child of God, a beginning of a new life in us, which is God's own life of grace brought to us by Jesus Christ. Jesus himself baptizes and makes us holy with the gifts of the Holy Spirit and impresses on our soul a character that cannot be taken away. Infants received Baptism—this same grace-filled gift from God that "does not presuppose any human merit"—from earliest times (see CCC 1282).

Three of the sacraments—Baptism, Confirmation, and Holy Orders—produce in the soul a mark that can never be lost. This mark, which is called a character, is a kind of badge of our membership in Christ, a sharing in his eternal priesthood, by which we are dedicated to sacred worship. These sacraments may be received only once.

(2) Baptism unites the new Christian so closely to Jesus that the person shares in his Death and Resurrection. Through this

sacrament the person dies to the old self, that is, the life of sin, and rises to new life, a life of grace.

(3) The result of Baptism is that a person is brought to peace with God: sins are forgiven, and the life of God is received.

(4) A person enters the Church by a new birth in Baptism. The new Christian becomes part of God's People and needs the company of fellow Christians to grow in faith and share in the continuing work of Jesus in the world.

84. What is Confirmation?

Confirmation is the sacrament by which those born again in Baptism now receive the seal of the Holy Spirit, the gift of the Father and the Son.

Confirmation strengthens the life of the Spirit received at Baptism. Jesus sends the Holy Spirit once more to Christian souls with new grace and new strength to lead the Christian life. The sign of Confirmation is made by the bishop as he extends his hands over the confirmed and prays that the Holy Spirit come upon them. This seal of the Spirit is the gift of the Father and the Son.

85. What does the seal of the Spirit do for us?

The seal of the Spirit prepares us to (1) be witnesses of Christ by a mature Christian life and (2) spread and defend the faith while living in the world.

(1) Confirmation unites the Christian more perfectly to the Church and gives the special strength of the Holy Spirit. This strength helps the Christian to live in the world as a witness of Christ and to serve others.

(2) A duty was placed upon us when we were confirmed: to bring Jesus Christ, his example, his way of life, and his Church to others. The strength of the grace of the Holy Spirit will help us to do so if we are generous enough to show some effort and to ask for his help in prayer.

86. What is Penance?

Penance is the sacrament that brings to the Christian God's merciful forgiveness for sins committed after Baptism.

In the Sacrament of Penance Jesus comes to forgive the sins of a baptized Christian, bringing the sinner consolation and peace.

Jesus gave the power of forgiving sins to his apostles when he appeared to them the evening of the day of his Resurrection. "Peace be with you," Jesus said to them again. "As the Father has sent me, so I send you." After saying this, he breathed on them and said, "Receive the Holy Spirit. If you forgive anyone's sins, they are forgiven. If you retain anyone's sins, they are retained" (Jn 20:21-23).

87. What are the effects of Penance?

Penance is (1) a means of obtaining pardon from God after a sincere confession, true sorrow, and the will not to sin again. (2) It brings about peace with the Church, which is wounded by our sins. (3) It helps us to work for holiness of life and to overcome habits of sin.

(1) The Sacrament of Penance is the means God gave us for his forgiveness of our sins. But we must be truly sorry for our sins, confess them to a priest, and receive absolution from the priest. We then do penance by saying the prayers or doing the good deeds assigned by the priest during confession. Outward signs of the sacrament by the sinner are these: (1) showing sorrow for sins committed; (2) confessing them; (3) willingly accepting the penance for them; and (4) receiving the absolution of the priest who says, "I absolve you from your sins in the name of the Father, and of the Son, ✠ and of the Holy Spirit."

(2) The Sacrament of Penance also brings about peace with the Church, which we have hurt by our sins.

(3) Through the Sacrament of Penance, Jesus, the Good Shepherd, forgives our sins and sends his Holy Spirit once more to

our soul with new grace and new strength to lead a better Christian life. We can join ourselves to Jesus, dying to sin and selfishness and rising with him to new life with God. Only with his help can we overcome temptation and avoid sin. Only with his grace can we practice virtue and become more like Jesus.

88. Is confession necessary if one has fallen into serious sin?

If one has fallen into serious sin, sacramental confession is the ordinary way established in the Church to bring about peace between the sinner and Christ and his Church.

Repentance and forgiveness of sins committed after Baptism are expressed in the Church through the Sacrament of Penance. It is the ordinary way offered by the Church to bring about peace with Christ and his Church. Since the life of Christians is filled with temptations and sins, this sacrament is open for them so that they may obtain pardon from the merciful God.

89. What is the effect of perfect sorrow for sin?

A sinner can also be restored to grace by perfect sorrow (contrition) for sin because he or she has offended God.

We have sorrow or contrition for our sins when we are sorry for them because they have offended the good God, our Father, and when we do not want to commit them again. Our sorrow is sincere when it comes from the heart. The real meaning of the virtue of Penance is hatred for sin as an offense against God who is all good and worthy of our love.

We should have contrition for mortal sin because it offends God seriously and keeps us from reaching heaven. It condemns us to eternal punishment. By true sorrow, we can be forgiven and receive God's grace again.

90. What is the wish of the Church concerning confession?

All Catholics, from their early years, should be instructed how to receive and best profit from the regular use of this sacrament.

The Church urges us to confess our sins with sincere sorrow in the Sacrament of Penance. She wishes us to use frequently those sacraments that help us to live a better Christian life, and the Sacrament of Penance is one of them. After Holy Eucharist, it is the one that can be received most frequently.

91. What is Holy Orders?

Holy Orders (1) makes certain members of the People of God like Christ the Mediator, (2) puts them in positions of special service in the Church, and (3) gives them a sacred power to carry out this service.

(1) Christ is the Mediator between us and the Father through his priesthood. He continues his sacrifice of the Cross in the Church at Holy Mass through his priests.

(2) Through this sacrament Jesus shares the work of his priesthood with other men—the bishops and the priests of the Catholic Church. Through them he makes himself present to offer the Sacrifice of the Mass, to baptize, to give the Sacrament of Confirmation, to give his Body and Blood in Holy Communion, to forgive sins in the Sacrament of Penance, to anoint the sick, and to bless marriages. The major orders of the Church are deacon, priest, and bishop.

(3) By his own authority, Jesus appointed the apostles to be his priests to carry on his work in the world. At the Last Supper he gave the apostles the power to change bread and wine into his Body and Blood in memory of him. After his Resurrection he gave them the power to forgive our sins. Before ascending into heaven he sent them to all nations to teach and baptize.

92. What special grace does Christ give in the Sacrament of Holy Orders?

Through this sacrament, Christ gives the special grace of the Holy Spirit to (1) guide and take care of those who believe, (2) proclaim and explain the Gospel, and (3) guide and sanctify God's people.

(1) Before he ascended into heaven, Jesus gave special instructions to his apostles. He wanted to be sure that there would be helpers to take care of his flock.

(2) Jesus sent his apostles to preach the Gospel of the New Covenant to every nation because he wanted to save all people.

(3) The apostles continued Christ's priestly work of being mediators between God and his people. They brought God's mercy and grace to the people and, in return, gave the people's praise to God. Christ was present, acting through them.

93. What can priests do as Christ's representatives?

Representing Christ, priests (1) offer the Sacrifice of the Mass, (2) administer the Sacrament of Penance for the forgiveness of sins, and (3) administer the Sacrament of the Anointing of the Sick.

(1) Knowing that the priesthood of Jesus and his Church was to be continued to the end of time, the apostles by ordaining priests and bishops passed on their priestly power to others. The most important work of the priest is the offering of the Sacrifice of the Mass. He acts in the name of Christ and in union with him as Jesus renews the sacrifice of the Cross in an unbloody way for the glory of God and the salvation of all.

(2) Through his priests Jesus forgives our sins and becomes, for all of us, a merciful high priest.

(3) Through his priests Jesus gives comfort to the suffering members of the Church and prepares them for their eternal union with God.

94. What is the Anointing of the Sick?

The Anointing of the Sick is the sacrament for the seriously ill, infirm, and aged.

Jesus showed a great love for sinners and the sick. He gave special care to the sick and cured them. He continues to come to the sick in the Sacrament of the Anointing of the Sick. The sign of this sacrament is the anointing with oil and the words of the priest. The priest anoints the forehead and then anoints the hands of the person receiving the sacrament.

95. When is this sacrament best received?

This sacrament is best received as soon as the danger of death begins from sickness or old age.

This sacrament is for those who are seriously sick. The sacrament can be repeated for persons who get well and become seriously ill again. Sorrow for sins is required to have sins forgiven.

96. What does the Church ask for by this anointing?

By this anointing and prayers, the Church through the priests asks the Lord (1) for possible restored health for the sick, (2) to lighten the sufferings of the sick, (3) to forgive their sins, and (4) to bring them to eternal salvation.

(1) Jesus comes to the sick in this sacrament and it may restore the sick person to health.

(2) Jesus gives graces to the sick which help them to bear the pain of their illness with patience.

(3) Jesus gives graces that help the sick to have deep sorrow for their sins, and this is needed for forgiveness.

(4) By this sacrament the sick or aged are prepared for entrance into the glory of heaven.

97. What does the Church encourage the sick to do?

The Church encourages the sick to help the People of God by offering their sufferings with the sufferings and Death of Jesus.

Since Jesus gives us his grace and divine life in this sacrament, he helps us to offer our sufferings in union with his own on the Cross that we might share in the work of the redemption. In this way, we can help the Church not only by making up for sin but also by meriting grace for the Church. If we share in the sufferings of Jesus, we can expect to share also in his glory.

Before the Sacrament of the Anointing of the Sick, the priest usually gives the sick person the Sacrament of Penance. After the anointing, he gives the Body and Blood of Christ.

A. FILL IN THE BLANKS

1. Baptism is the sacrament of (1) .... made holy by ...., (2) unity with Jesus in ...., (3) cleansing from ...., and (4) welcome into ....(83)
2. Confirmation is the sacrament by which .... now receive ...., the gift of .... (84)
3. The seal of the Spirit prepares us to (1) be.................................... by a mature .... and (2) .... while living in the world. (85)
4. Penance is the sacrament that brings to the Christian .... for sins committed .... (86)
5. Penance is a means of .... after................. ....(87)
6. Penance brings about ...., which is wounded by ...., and it helps us ....and to ....(87)
7. If one has fallen into serious sin, sacramental confession is .... to bring about .... (88)
8. A sinner can also be restored to grace .... because he or she has .... (89)

9. All Catholics, from their early years, should be instructed how .... and .... from the .... of the Sacrament of Penance. (90)
10. Holy Orders (1) makes certain members of the People of God ...., (2) puts them in positions .... in the Church, and (3) gives them ....(91)
11. Through the Sacrament of Holy Orders, Christ gives.................. .... to (1) ...., (2) ...., and (3) .... (92)
12. Representing Christ, priests (1) offer ...., (2) administer the Sacrament of..., and (3) administer the Sacrament of .... (93)
13. The Anointing of the Sick is ....(94)
14. The Anointing of the Sick is best received .... from .... (95)
15. By the anointing and prayers, the Church asks the Lord (1) for ...., (2) to lighten ...., (3) to forgive ...., and (4) to bring them to .... (96)
16. The Church encourages the sick to ....by offering their sufferings with ....(97)

B. BIBLE READING John 20:19-23

Jesus Appears to the Disciples

On the evening of that same day [when Jesus rose from the dead], the first day of the week, the doors of the house where the disciples had gathered were locked because of their fear of the Jews. Jesus then came and stood in their midst and said to them, "Peace be with you." After saying this, he showed them his hands and his side.

The disciples were filled with joy when they saw the Lord. "Peace be with you," Jesus said to them again. "As the Father has sent me, so I send you."

After saying this, he breathed on them and said, "Receive the Holy Spirit. If you forgive anyone's sins, they are forgiven. If you retain anyone's sins, they are retained."

Discussion:

1. Why did the disciples lock the door after Jesus died?
2. How did Jesus greet his disciples?
3. How did the disciples feel when they saw Jesus?
4. What did Jesus say to his disciples?
5. Why did Jesus breathe on them?
6. What power did Jesus give his apostles?
7. How is this power used today?

C. PRACTICE

1. We should often ask the Holy Spirit to give us the graces offered us through our Confirmation, especially the grace to overcome temptation to sin, and the grace to be a good example in living our Christian faith so that we may be witnesses of Christ in the world.
2. We should examine our conscience every day. Just before retiring at night, we should make an effort to recall the sins we have committed during the day and then make an act of contrition for these as well as all our past sins.
3. The Church wishes us to use the Sacrament of Penance frequently, once each month, or more often if we can, so that we may overcome our habits of sin and receive the grace we need to live a better Christian life.

JESUS SPEAKS:

"Peace I leave with you, my peace I give to you. Not as the world gives do I give it to you." (Jn 14:27)

CHAPTER

16 The Holy Eucharist

98. Why is the Eucharist the center of all sacramental life?

The Eucharist is the center of all sacramental life because it is of the greatest importance for uniting and strengthening the Church.

Of all the sacraments, the most important is the Sacrament of Holy Eucharist. Jesus Christ is present in the Holy Eucharist to be our sacrifice, our food, our life, our companion to strengthen and nourish us with his Body and Blood. He comes to us to unite us with himself and with all the members of the Church.

99. Why is the Eucharistic celebration carried out?

The Eucharistic celebration is carried out in obedience to the words of Jesus at the Last Supper: "Do this in memory of me" (Luke 22:19).

At the Last Supper Jesus gave bread and wine to his apostles to eat and drink, telling them that it was his own Body and Blood. He then asked them to remember him always by doing this same thing among themselves.

The Mass is the Church's way of doing what Jesus did at the Last Supper. Jesus gave the apostles the command and the power to bring the Eucharist to us when he said, "Do this in memory of me."

100. What happens when a priest speaks the words of Eucharistic consecration?

When a priest pronounces the words of Eucharistic consecration, the bread and wine are changed into the Body and Blood of Christ, given in sacrifice.

His words and power made Jesus really present in the bread and wine that he gave his apostles to eat. They actually received Jesus in that meal and were united with him. This made the apostles one with Jesus and all he did. They shared his gift of himself to his Father on the Cross, for he was given in sacrifice. The apostles then gave Christ to the People of God in the Eucharist.

101. How is Christ present in the Eucharist?

Christ himself, true God and true man, is truly and substantially present under the appearances of bread and wine.

When Jesus gave the apostles his Body, the Body looked like bread and even tasted like bread, but it was not bread; it was his Body for he said so. When he gave the apostles his Blood, the Blood appeared to be wine and even tasted like wine, but it was not wine; it was his Blood for he said so. This holy sacrament looks like bread and tastes like bread, but it is not bread: it is Jesus. To come to us Jesus covers himself with the appearances of bread and wine. We cannot understand this, but we take the word of God that it is so. The Eucharist is called the Mystery of Faith.

All priests in the Catholic Church have the power to change bread and wine into the Body and Blood of Christ. In the Eucharist it is Christ himself who consecrates through the priest as the words of consecration are said, "This is my Body.... This is the chalice of my Blood."

102. What is the Sacrifice of the Mass?

(1) The Sacrifice of the Mass is not only a ritual that reminds us of the Sacrifice of Calvary. (2) In it, through the ministry of priests, Christ continues till the end of time the sacrifice of the Cross in an unbloody manner.

(1) At the Last Supper, Jesus instituted the Eucharistic sacrifice of his Body and Blood to continue for all time the sacrifice of the Cross until he would come again. He gave his Church a remembrance of his Death and Resurrection.

(2) But the Mass is also a true sacrifice. Through the hands of priests and in the name of the whole Church, the sacrifice of Jesus is offered in the Eucharist in an unbloody and sacramental way. The priest, by the sacred power he receives from Christ, and acting in the person of Christ, brings about the Eucharistic sacrifice and offers it to God in the name of all the people.

The Mass is a sacrifice in which the Church not only remembers Jesus but really brings him and his saving Death and Resurrection into the present so that his followers may become part of it. When the Church celebrates the Eucharist, Jesus is truly there. It is he who does once more what he did at the Last Supper.

103. What is Holy Communion?

The Eucharist is also a meal that (1) reminds us of the Last Supper, (2) celebrates our unity in Christ, and (3) makes present the messianic banquet of the kingdom of heaven.

(1) Jesus nourishes our soul with himself, the Bread of Life. He offered himself as a sacrifice on the Cross. In Holy Communion we partake of the Body that was given in death for us, the Blood

that was shed for our salvation. This holy meal reminds us of what happened at the Last Supper when Jesus told his apostles to do this in memory of him.

(2) Communion nourishes us with the life of God and unites us to Jesus and to one another. In drawing us to union with Jesus, our heavenly Father draws us closer to each other because we share in the divine life of Jesus through his grace. The Holy Eucharist not only is a sign of the unity and love that bind us to Jesus and each other but also gives us the grace we need to make that love strong and sincere.

(3) Holy Communion gives us a foretaste of the banquet of Christ in the kingdom of heaven because it is the same Son of God made man who will be united with us in a union of joy forever in heaven. Jesus also promised that our body would some day enjoy his presence. He said, "Whoever feeds upon my flesh and drinks my blood has eternal life, and I will raise him up on the last day" (Jn 6:54). The meal, prepared for us by God the Father, makes us ready to take part in that heavenly communion with Jesus and his Father.

104. What does Jesus do for Christians in the Eucharist?

In the Eucharist Jesus nourishes Christians with his own self, the Bread of Life, so that they may become a people more pleasing to God and filled with greater love of God and neighbor.

Holy Communion is Jesus Christ himself under the appearances of bread and wine uniting himself to Christians to nourish their souls. Jesus said, "I am the living bread that came down from heaven. Whoever eats this bread will live forever; and the bread that I will give is my flesh, for the life of the world" (Jn 6:51).

Holy Communion helps us to love God more because of the divine grace that grows in our souls. This same grace helps us to love others for the love of God. Jesus strengthens us through actual or sacramental grace that we may overcome temptation and avoid sinning against God and our neighbor. Only by the help of his grace can we truly live a life of charity and fulfill his greatest commandment.

105. What must we do to receive the Eucharist worthily?

To receive the Eucharist worthily, we must be in the state of grace.

As long as we are in the state of grace, we are prepared to receive Jesus each time that we are present at the Holy Sacrifice of the Mass, because his Body, the food of this sacrificial meal, is for us the way to eternal life. The best way to prepare our soul for union with Jesus in Holy Communion is to offer him and to offer ourselves with him to God the Father in the Sacrifice of the Mass. Confession is not necessary before Holy Communion unless we have a serious sin to confess, but we should receive the Sacrament of Penance faithfully, each month or more often, if we wish.

106. Why is the Eucharist a sacrament of unity?

The Eucharist is a sacrament of unity because it unites the faithful more closely with God and with one another.

By eating the Body of the Lord, we are brought into a close union with him and with one another. St. Paul said, "Because there is one bread, we who are many are one body, for we all partake of the one bread" (1 Cor 10:17).

107. Why is the Eucharist reserved in our churches?

The Eucharist is reserved in our churches to be a powerful help to prayer and the service of others.

Reservation of the Blessed Sacrament means that at the end of Communion the remaining consecrated Bread is placed in the tabernacle and reverently reserved. The Eucharist reserved is a

continuing sign of our Lord's Real Presence among his people and spiritual food for the sick and dying.

108. What do we owe Christ in the Blessed Sacrament reserved?

We owe gratitude, adoration, and devotion to the Real Presence of Christ in the Blessed Sacrament reserved.

We must show gratitude, adoration, and devotion to the Real Presence of Christ. We demonstrate these practices in our visits to the tabernacle in our churches and in Benediction. Benediction is a devotion in which the Blessed Sacrament is exposed to the people for reverence and adoration. The priest blesses the people with the Lord's Body.

A. FILL IN THE BLANKS

1. The Eucharist is the center of ....because it is of the greatest importance for ....(98)
2. The Eucharistic celebration is carried out in obedience to ....(99)
3. When a priest pronounces the words of Eucharistic consecration, the bread and wine ....(100)
4. Christ himself, true God and true man, is .... present under the appearances of .... (101)
5. (1) The Sacrifice of the Mass is not only a .... (2) In it, through the ministry ...., Christ continues till the end of time .... (102)
6. The Eucharist is also a .... that (1) reminds us of ...., (2) celebrates ...., and (3) makes present ....of the kingdom of heaven. (103)
7. In the Eucharist Jesus nourishes Christians with .... so that they may become ....and filled with .... (104)
8. To receive the Eucharist worthily, we must ....(105)
9. The Eucharist is a sacrament of unity because ....(106)

10. The Eucharist is reserved in our churches to be a powerful help .... (107)
11. We owe ....to the Real Presence of Christ in the Blessed Sacrament reserved. (108)

B. BIBLE READING

John 6:26-69

The Promise of the Holy Eucharist

One day Jesus fed a crowd of about five thousand with five barley loaves and two fish, and the next day, the crowd looked for him in Capernaum.

Jesus said to them, "You came looking for me not because you have seen signs but because you ate the loaves and your hunger was satisfied. Do not work for food that perishes but for the food that endures for eternal life, which the Son of Man will give you."

"Sir," they begged him, "give us this bread always."

Jesus answered them, "I am the living bread that came down from heaven. Whoever eats this bread will live forever; and the bread that I will give is my flesh, for the life of the world."

Then the Jews started to argue among themselves, saying, "How can this man give us his flesh to eat?"

Jesus said to them, "Amen, amen, I say to you, unless you eat the flesh of the Son of Man and drink his blood, you do not have life within you. Whoever feeds upon my flesh and drinks my blood has eternal life, and I will raise him up on the last day. For my flesh is real food, and my blood is real drink. Whoever feeds upon my flesh and drinks my blood dwells in me and I dwell in him.

After hearing his words, many of his disciples said, "This is a hard saying. Who can accept it?" Many of them turned away and no longer remained with him.

Then Jesus said to the Twelve, "Do you also wish to leave?"

Simon Peter answered him, "Lord, to whom shall we go? You have the words of eternal life. We have come to believe and know that you are the Holy One of God."

Discussion:

1. What did Jesus say about himself as the living bread from heaven?
2. Why did the Jews argue over the words of Jesus?
3. What did Jesus say in answer to the Jews?
4. Why did the Jews begin to depart?
5. What did Peter say when Jesus asked him whether he wanted to leave him or not?
6. What do the words of Jesus on the Eucharist tell us about Holy Communion?

Matthew 26:26-28

The Institution of the Eucharist

On the night before he died, Jesus took his place at table along with the apostles. He said to them, "I have eagerly desired to eat this Passover with you before I suffer. For I tell you that from this moment on I shall never eat it again until it is fulfilled in the kingdom of God."

During the supper Jesus told his apostles many important things. He gave them a new commandment: love one another. He promised to send them the Holy Spirit. He asked them to remain united with him. He prayed to his Father for them. Most importantly, he gave them the Holy Eucharist for all of us by instituting the Sacrifice of the Mass.

The Last Supper

While they were eating, Jesus took bread, and after he had pronounced the blessing, he broke it and gave it to his disciples, saying, "Take this and eat; this is my body." Then he took a cup, and after offering thanks he gave it to them, saying, "Drink from this, all of you. For this is my blood of the covenant, which will be shed on behalf of many for the forgiveness of sins. Do this in memory of me."

The Eucharist is a memorial of our Lord's Passion and Death. This Flesh which he gave to his apostles to eat was the Flesh of the sacrificial Victim who would offer himself on the Cross; this Blood was the Blood that was to be shed for our redemption on Calvary. By giving us the Mass, Jesus made it possible for us to be present at the Sacrifice of Calvary, which is now reenacted on the altar in an unbloody manner. In Holy Communion we receive the Victim of Calvary as food for the nourishment of our souls. Jesus left this gift of himself for the end as his deathbed gift of love. We must love him in return by appreciating the Mass and Holy Communion.

Discussion:

1. When did Jesus institute the Blessed Sacrament of the Altar?
2. What did Jesus do at the Last Supper?
3. Why is the Eucharist a memorial of our Lord's Passion and Death?
4. Why is the Mass the same sacrifice that Jesus offered on the Cross?
5. How must we show our love for the Holy Eucharist?

C. PRACTICE

1. The people at the time of our Lord could see his face, could hear his voice, could feel the touch of his hand as he blessed them. Though we cannot see him with the eyes of the body, we have the greater privilege of receiving his sacred Body, of eating his Flesh, and drinking his Blood. By means of the Holy Eucharist, his greatest gift to us, we have his lasting presence among us. We should share in the sacrificial meal of Holy Communion at least each Sunday or Saturday evening, and during the week if we can, so that we may grow in the love of Christ and in his grace.
2. When, for some reason, we are unable to receive Holy Communion we should make a "spiritual communion" any time of the day, that is, desire to be united with Jesus in sincere love.

CHAPTER

17 The Sacrament of Matrimony

109. Who instituted marriage?

Marriage was instituted by the Creator himself with certain purposes, laws, and blessings given by him.

At the very beginning of the human race, when he created Adam and Eve, God instituted marriage. We read in the Book of Genesis: "God created mankind in his image, in the image of God he created them, male and female he created them. God blessed them and told them, 'Be fruitful and multiply, and fill the earth; subdue it'" (Gen 1:27-28).

110. Who raised marriage to the dignity of a sacrament?

Christ raised marriage of the baptized to the dignity of a sacrament.

Jesus Christ made marriage a lifelong, sacred union of husband and wife by which they give themselves to each other and to him. He raised this union to the dignity of a sacrament for the baptized.

111. Who are the ministers of the sacrament?

The spouses, expressing their personal and lasting consent, are the ministers of the sacrament.

The husband is the minister of God's grace to the wife and the wife to the husband. The priest officiates at the ceremony as the Church's witness to this act of grace.

112. In what do we see the dignity of the sacrament?

(1) The spouses live together in Christ's grace, (2) they imitate Christ's own love for his Church, and (3) they are consecrated to live up to the dignity of matrimony and to carry out its duties.

(1) In the Sacrament of Matrimony Christ comes to man and wife to live with them, to give them his grace, and to help them fulfill their rights and duties to God, to each other, and to their children faithfully until death.

(2) St. Paul tells us that marriage is a sign of union of Jesus and his Church. "Husbands, love your wives, just as Christ loved the Church and gave himself up for her in order to sanctify her. . . . This is a great mystery. Here I am applying it to Christ and the Church" (Eph 5:25, 32). He describes the Church as the bride of Christ, made beautiful by her spouse. Jesus offered his life for his bride to make her holy.

(3) The sacrament gives sanctifying grace, the divine life, and all the actual graces needed throughout married life to bring about an ever deeper union of man and wife in soul and body so that they may live up to what they promised in their marriage vows and in their vocation of parenthood.

113. Why was marriage instituted?

Marriage was instituted (1) to bring children into the world and to educate them and (2) for the strong, loving companionship of the spouses.

(1) From married love come children. In his love for us God gives us life and the care we need as children from parents.

(2) From marriage a man and his wife have a loving companionship that is stronger than any other in life. The Lord God said: "This is why a man leaves his father and his mother and joins with a wife, and the two become one flesh" (Gen 2:24).

114. How long does the bond of marriage last?

The bond of marriage lasts until the death of one of the spouses, thereby echoing Jesus' words of its permanence: "What God has joined together, let no one separate" (Mk 10:9).

This being said, the *Catechism* teaches that although "*Divorce* is a grave offense against the natural law" (CCC 2384) and "immoral also because it introduces disorder into the family and into society" (CCC 2385), it also teaches that "If civil divorce remains the only possible way of ensuring certain legal rights, the care of the children, or the protection of inheritance, it can be tolerated and does not constitute a moral offense" (CCC 2383).

115. What is the calling of every family?

The calling of every family is to share life together with a deep, personal love according to God's will.

It is the family's calling to become a community, sharing life together in deep love. The family is the most sacred of all societies. Our character, beliefs, thoughts, and virtues come from good loving parents.

116. What is the aim of family life?

Family life has this aim: that the spouses be ready with generous hearts to work together with the love of the Creator who through them will enlarge and enrich his own family day by day.

Marriage is a lifelong partnership of love. The giving of self in marriage brings children who make the love of husbands and wives richer and fulfills one of the purposes of marriage. If

husbands and wives are generous to God in working with him according to his will, enlarging his own family on earth, he will bless them in this life and especially in heaven.

A. FILL IN THE BLANKS

1. Marriage was instituted by .... with certain .... given by him. (109)
2. Christ raised marriage of the baptized to the dignity .... (110)
3. The ministers of the Sacrament of Matrimony are ....(111)
4. The dignity of the Sacrament of Matrimony shows itself in that the spouses (1) live together ...., (2) imitate Christ's own love for ...., and (3) are consecrated to .... and to ....(112)
5. Marriage was instituted (1) to .... and (2) for ....(113)
6. The bond of marriage lasts until ....(114)
7. The calling of every family is to ....(115)
8. Family life has this aim: that the spouses be ready with generous hearts to .... (116)

B. BIBLE READING

John 2:1-11

The Marriage at Cana

Jesus went with his disciples to a town in Galilee called Cana to attend a wedding. The Mother of Jesus was at this wedding as well. Before the wedding feast was over, there was no more wine. Mary understood this embarrassing situation. She believed that her Son had the power to do whatever he wished, and she said to him, "They have no wine."

Jesus responded, "Woman, what concern is this to us? My hour has not yet come." Jesus meant that it was not yet time for so public a miracle.

Since his Mother knew that Jesus would in some way help the people in their need, she said to the servants, "Do whatever he tells you."

Nearby there were six large stone jars, each holding twenty to thirty gallons. Jesus said to the servants, "Fill the jars with water."

The servants obeyed Jesus and filled the jars up to the brim. Once they were filled, Jesus said, "Now draw some and take it to the chief steward."

They did as Jesus said and saw that it had been turned into wine. Since the chief steward did not know where the servants had gotten the wine, he called over the bridegroom and said, "Everyone serves the choice wine first, and then an inferior vintage when the guests have been drinking for a while. However, you have saved the best wine until now."

Mary said to Jesus, "They have no wine."

Jesus performed this first miracle, thereby revealing his glory, and his disciples believed in him.

Discussion:

1. What did the Mother of Jesus do when she saw that there was no more wine?
2. How many stone jars were there and how much did each jar hold?
3. What did Jesus tell the servants to do?
4. What happened to the water in the jars?
5. What does this miracle teach us about the power of Mary's prayers?
6. What does this miracle have to do with marriage?

C. PRACTICE

1. The graces of the Sacrament of Marriage are given to be used in the daily life of a Christian husband, wife, and family. Parents and children should receive the Sacraments of Penance and Holy Eucharist often. It is important that they receive them with their state of life in mind, seeking by means of confession to rid themselves of the faults that interfere with a happy family life and by means of Holy Communion to grow in love for one another in Christ.
2. Children should pray for their parents and their siblings that they may share life together with a sincere personal love according to God's will. They should do all they can to bring this about by love, respect, patience, and obedience.

JESUS SPEAKS:

"Amen, I say to you, unless you change and become like little children, you will never enter the kingdom of heaven. Whoever humbles himself and becomes like this child is the greatest in the kingdom of heaven." (Mt 18:3-4)

Part Seven — SIN

CHAPTER

18 The Sins of Human Beings

117. What is our greatest problem in working out our salvation?

In working out our salvation, our greatest problem is sin.

Working out our salvation means doing God's will. Sinners want to live without regard for God's will. They choose whatever they think will make them happy, even though it does not fit into God's plan for them. They do not trust God's love for them.

118. How was original sin committed?

(1) God made man in a state of holiness, but man abused his liberty at the urging of the Evil One. (2) He set himself against God and looked for happiness apart from him.

(1) Man was the crown of God's creation; of all on earth he alone could give back to God the love that God first gave him. God wanted mankind to live as his family, united to each other and to himself in love. Nothing was to disturb this family: not sickness, death, ignorance, or weakness.

(2) But Adam abused his liberty. He disobeyed and rejected God's care. He wanted to search for happiness in his own way.

119. How are we born in original sin?

We are born in original sin because fallen human nature—stripped of the grace that clothed it, hurt in its natural powers, and subjected to death—was carried on to all of us.

When Adam sinned, he cut himself off from God. He was stripped of the grace God had given him. His human nature was harmed in its natural powers. Sickness and death entered his life. Adam's descendants were to suffer in the same way. We are born into this world separated from our loving Father and subject to death. The main sign of sin in the world is our rejection of God. Other signs are war, poverty, hunger, hatred of people, violence, and other injustices.

120. What is personal sin?

Personal sin is committed by a person who, acting knowingly and willingly, breaks the moral law.

Sin is willful disobedience to God. This disobedience may be an action, a thought, a desire, an intention, or an omission.

121. What happens when the sinner commits a personal sin?

The sinner who commits a personal sin (1) fails in love of God, (2) turns away from the goal of doing God's will, and (3) breaks the relationship with the Father by serious offense (mortal sin).

(1) The sinner fails in love of God because of a willingness to turn against God.

(2) The sinner chooses to do his or her own will rather than God's will and is willing to displease God and even lose his friendship.

(3) Serious or mortal sin is a rejection of God that destroys the life shared between God and the sinner. It is a serious violation of the law of God.

A small violation of the law of God (venial sin) does not take away God's life from the soul or break God's friendship, but it weakens our love for God and harms ourselves and others.

The effect of mortal sin is separation from God and damage to ourselves and others. If we do not wish to change and continue to refuse to do what God wants us to do, the separation from God lasts. The Church calls this permanent separation from God "hell."

122. What must the Christian have to commit a sin?

To commit a sin the Christian must (1) have clear knowledge of right and wrong and (2) be able to choose with an informed conscience to love God and avoid offending him.

(1) The person who commits the sin must know what is being done and that what is being done is an offense against God.

(2) There must be full consent of the will in the case of a serious sin.

123. What must we believe concerning God's forgiveness?

We must believe that God (1) is merciful and will pardon the sinner who is truly sorry and (2) by the power of his grace will draw the sinner to salvation.

(1) Only God can forgive our sins. He chose his Son to be the one to suffer and to die for our sins. Jesus is called our Savior because he saved us from sin. God will pardon us if we are truly sorry for our sins and want to change our sinful ways. We can always look to God for merciful forgiveness.

(2) In the Sacrament of Penance Jesus forgives our sins and gives us the peace that belongs to God's children. He also gives

us his grace to overcome sin in the future. He gives us the strength to be faithful to God's law of love. Through his grace he draws us to salvation.

A. FILL IN THE BLANKS

1. In working out our salvation our greatest problem is ....(117)
2. Original sin was committed because (1) man abused his............. at the urging of .... (2) He set himself against .... and looked for happiness apart from .... (118)
3. We are born in original sin because fallen human nature—stripped of ...., hurt in ...., and subjected to ....—was carried on to ....(119)
4. Personal sin is committed by a person who,...........................(120)
5. The sinner who commits a personal sin (1) fails in ...., (2) turns away from ...., and (3) breaks the relationship .... (121)
6. To commit a sin the Christian must (1) have .... and (2) be able to .... to love God and avoid offending him. (122)
7. We must believe that God (1) is merciful and will .... and (2) by the power of his grace will .... (123)

B. BIBLE READING Luke 15:11-32

The Prodigal Son

There was a man who had two sons. The younger of them said to his father, "Father, give me the share of your estate that I will inherit." And so the father divided the property between them.

The younger son gathered together everything he had and traveled to a distant country, where he squandered his inheritance.

When he had spent it all, a severe famine afflicted that country, and he began to be in need. So he went and hired himself out to one of the local inhabitants who sent him to his farm to feed the pigs. He would have willingly filled his stomach with the pods that the pigs were eating, but no one gave him anything.

Then he came to his senses and said, "How many of my father's hired workers have more food than they can consume, while here I am, dying of hunger. I will depart from this place and go to my father, and I will say to him, 'Father, I have sinned against heaven and

against you. I am no longer worthy to be called your son. Treat me like one of your hired workers.' "

So he set out for his father's house. But while he was still a long way off, his father saw him and was filled with compassion. He ran to him, threw his arms around him, and kissed him. Then the son said to him, "Father, I have sinned against heaven and against you. I am no longer worthy to be called your son."

But the father said to his servants, "Quickly bring out the finest robe we have and put it on him. Place a ring on his finger and sandals on his feet. Then bring the fatted calf and kill it, and let us celebrate with a feast. For this son of mine was dead and has come back to life. He was lost, and now he has been found." And they began to celebrate.

The elder son returned from the fields, learned that his brother had come home, and heard the celebration going on. He became angry and refused to go into the house.

His father came out and began to plead with him, but he said to his father in reply, "All these years I have worked like a slave for you, and I never once disobeyed your orders. Even so, you have never even given me a young goat so that I might celebrate with my friends.

But when this son of yours returns after wasting his inheritance from you..., you kill the fatted calf for him."

Then the father said to him, "Son, you are with me always, and everything I have is yours. But it was only right that we should celebrate and rejoice, because this brother of yours was dead and has come to life; he was lost and now he has been found."

Discussion:

1. What did the younger son ask his father to do for him?
2. What happened to the younger son after he left his father?
3. What happened when the younger son came home?
4. What did the father tell the servants to do?
5. What did the older son say to his father?
6. What answer did the father give his older son?
7. What does this story teach us about the Sacrament of Penance?

C. PRACTICE

1. Since mortal sin is treated so lightly by the world, we must always strive to keep alive in ourselves a real hatred of it. We can do this by remembering the sufferings and Death of Jesus Christ, the price for the mortal sins of men.
2. In order to avoid mortal sin we must try to avoid even less serious sins. If we are faithful to God in smaller things, we shall be faithful to him in more serious things. We should pray for help from God when we are tempted to sin. If we do so, God will always give us strength to overcome temptation. In order to avoid sin we also must avoid any person, place or thing that may lead us into sin.

JESUS SPEAKS:

"Anyone who wishes to follow me must deny himself, take up his cross, and follow me." (Mt 16:24)

"Pray that you may not enter into temptation." (Lk 22:40)

"What will it profit a man if he gains the whole world and forfeits his very life? Or what can he give in exchange for his life?" (Mt 16:26)

Part Eight — THE LIFE OF GRACE

CHAPTER 19 The New Life in the Spirit

124. What happens when we accept the Spirit of Christ?

When we accept the Spirit of Christ, God leads us to a new way of life.

All Persons of the Blessed Trinity have a part in the holy work of getting and giving grace to people. The work of giving grace is especially the work of the Holy Spirit because it is a work of love, and the Holy Spirit is the Spirit of Love of the Father and the Son. He makes souls holy through the gift of grace.

125. What does this new way of life do for us?

This new way of life gives us the power to (1) share in God's own life and (2) be joined to the Father and to Christ in a union of love that not even death can break.

(1) The Spirit brings God's life to us and all that we do so that a person is said to live in the "state of grace." Grace is God's gift of himself from which comes our life in God, which is the life of grace.

This new life gives us the power to share in God's own life by the virtues of faith, hope, and love. Faith is a free gift by which

the Holy Spirit helps us to accept God's word and to realize that God loves us and cares for us and that we can count on him. We can hope because in Jesus Christ, God has promised us his love and care forever and that he will never leave us if only we remain united with him. Charity is the love of God and of others because they too belong to God. The presence in us of the Holy Spirit means that we are able to love even our enemies with the love of God.

(2) Grace is God's gift of himself. By grace we are united to the Father and to Christ in a union of love. Jesus said, "Whoever loves me will keep my word, and my Father will love him, and we will come to him and make our abode with him" (Jn 14:23).

126. What does the indwelling Holy Spirit give us?

The indwelling Holy Spirit (1) gives us hope and courage, (2) heals our weakness of soul, (3) helps us overcome our evil desires and selfishness, (4) helps us practice virtues such as love and patience, and (5) makes our prayer more pleasing to God.

(1) Through sanctifying grace and the powers of faith, hope, and love that come with it as well as through actual grace (the help we need for mind and will to be good), we are made holy by the Holy Spirit who lives in our soul. His presence gives us the hope that God will grant us the help we need to save our soul and live with God forever in heaven; at the same time his presence gives us the courage and strength we need to accept the suffering and troubles of life.

(2) The Holy Spirit gives us actual grace, that special help that gives light to our mind and strength to our will to do good and to avoid evil.

(3) Evil persons, places, and things in this world can lead us into sin. The desires of our body also tempt us to do things unworthy of a Christian such as impurity, laziness, gluttony,

anger, envy, pride, and neglect of our neighbor's needs. We need the help of the Holy Spirit to lead a good Christian life.

(4) Only when we allow the Holy Spirit to guide us in the practice of virtue and when we use the help of his grace can we continue to share in God's divine life of grace and live as his children.

(5) The Holy Spirit unites us with God by love and helps us to keep our friendship with him by prayer. He makes our prayer more pleasing to God because through the grace of the Holy Spirit our life is also more pleasing to God.

127. What is sanctifying grace?

Sanctifying grace is a habitual gift of God that makes us holy and pleasing to him.

By sanctifying grace our soul shares in the very life of God even while we are on this earth. Grace makes us holy and pleasing to God because it helps us to live as his obedient children.

128. What does grace do for us?

Through grace the Holy Spirit helps us to (1) die to sin, (2) share in the divinity of the Son of God by helping us live as children of God, and (3) be closely united with the Most Holy Trinity by love.

(1) With the help of the grace of the Holy Spirit we are able to die to sin and live to God. We receive the strength we need to sacrifice ourselves by avoiding everything that would lead us into sin. With his help we can overcome our desires to do whatever might be against God's commandments.

(2) By grace we share in the divine life of the Son of God because we are adopted children of God. We became God's children in Baptism when for the first time we received the new life of grace.

(3) St. Paul reminds Christians that they are the temple of God. "Do you not realize that you are God's temple, and that the Spirit of God dwells in you?" (1 Cor 3:16). The Holy Spirit was sent in order that he might make the Church holy. Through him, the Father gives life to those of us who are willing to give up sin, because he is the Spirit of life. United in Jesus as his followers, we are led by the Holy Spirit in our journey to the kingdom of our heavenly Father. He helps us to fulfill our duties. He prompts us to strive for what is good. He encourages us to pray. His grace unites us to the Most Holy Trinity by love.

129. What has God willed for our salvation?

God has willed that we (1) receive the sanctifying grace of adoption as God's children and (2) gain eternal life.

(1) Our greatest honor is to be children of God. St. Paul says, "Those who are led by the Spirit of God are children of God" (Rom 8:14). Grace is God's gift to us. We could never have earned it. Jesus bought grace for all of us by his suffering and Death and Resurrection. We had no right to grace.

(2) Through grace we also can gain eternal life. Through the merits of the Death and Resurrection of Jesus we hope to be united with God forever.

130. What is our greatest dignity?

Our greatest dignity is to have supernatural life because of the grace of Christ the Savior.

We received two lives from God. One is the natural life we received at birth. The other is the supernatural life we received when we were baptized as Christians. Jesus said to Nicodemus, "Amen, amen, I say to you, no one can see the kingdom of God without being born from above" (Jn 3:3). We obtain natural life from our father and mother; we obtain supernatural life from God our Father. St. John

says, "See what love the Father has bestowed on us, enabling us to be called children of God, and that is what we are" (1 Jn 3:1).

Our greatest honor is to be children of God and to have God's life in our soul because of the grace of Christ, our Savior. We must try to live a holy life and train ourselves to keep God's grace as our most precious treasure. We must ask the Holy Spirit to help us live according to our great dignity as children of God and as true Christians.

A. FILL IN THE BLANKS

1. When we accept the Spirit of Christ, God leads us to .... (124)
2. This new way of life gives us the power to (1) ....and (2) be joined to .... in a union of .... (125)
3. The indwelling Holy Spirit (1) gives us ...., (2) heals ...., (3) helps us overcome ...., (4) helps us practice virtues such as ...., and (5) .... more pleasing to God. (126)
4. Sanctifying grace is .... that makes us ....(127)
5. Through grace the Holy Spirit helps us to (1) die to ...., (2) share in .... by helping us .... (3) be closely united ....(128)
6. God has willed that we (1) receive .... and (2) gain .... (129)
7. Our greatest dignity is .... because of ....(130)

B. BIBLE READING John 3:1-21

Nicodemus

There was a man from the Pharisees named Nicodemus, a member of the Jewish ruling council, who came to Jesus at night. "Rabbi," he said, "we know that you are a teacher who has come from God, for no one would be able to perform the signs that you do unless God were with him."

Jesus replied, "Amen, amen, I say to you, no one can see the kingdom of God without being born from above."

Nicodemus asked, "How can a man be born again once he is old? Is it possible for him to enter a second time into his mother's womb and be born?"

Jesus talks to Nicodemus.

Jesus said, "Amen, amen, I say to you, no one can enter the kingdom of God unless he is born of water and the Spirit. What is born of the flesh is flesh, and what is born of the Spirit is spirit. You should not be astonished when I say, 'You must be born from above.' The wind blows where it chooses, and you hear the sound of it, but you do not know where it comes from or where it goes. So it is with everyone who is born of the Spirit."

Jesus was saying that if we believe in him, the Holy Spirit gives us a new life. We are "born again." We become children of God. We cannot understand how the Holy Spirit gives us this new life, just as we cannot understand how the wind blows.

Jesus continued to teach Nicodemus: "For God so loved the world that he gave his only Son, so that everyone who believes in him may not perish but may attain eternal life."

Nicodemus was a good man. He kept the law of God carefully. But that was not enough to open the way into the kingdom of God.

Unless the Holy Spirit gives us a new life, we cannot see the kingdom of God. We call this life sanctifying grace, which is God's life in us. We receive this grace for the first time in Baptism.

Nicodemus listened carefully. He had never heard such wonderful words. He could not understand. But when he went away he thought about it. And after a while he did believe in Jesus. He was born again, and he became a child of God.

Discussion:

1. Who was Nicodemus?
2. Why did Nicodemus come to Jesus?
3. What did Jesus tell Nicodemus?
4. Did Nicodemus believe in Jesus?
5. How do the words of Jesus explain the grace of God and the Holy Spirit?
6. Why do the words of Jesus refer to Baptism?

C. PRACTICE

1. Since grace, which is a share in the life of God, is a free gift from God to which we have no right, we should show that it means a great deal to us. We do this by avoiding everything that may be sinful, for this may put us in danger of losing God's grace. We should make frequent use of the Sacraments of Penance and Holy Eucharist, through which we can grow in God's grace. We should pray often, for prayer helps us to continue in this life of God and brings us many actual graces (or help from God), which are light for our mind and strength for our will.

I am the Way, the Truth and the Life

Part Nine — THE MORAL LIFE

CHAPTER 20 Human and Christian Freedom

131. What is God's plan concerning freedom?

God's plan is that we, united with Jesus Christ, should give a free answer to God's call.

It is part of our dignity and duty to be free, since we are responsible for our actions. We must keep the law of God taught by Jesus. We must be free to answer God's call. We can do so with the help of Jesus Christ.

132. How was freedom harmed?

At the beginning, God gave the gift of freedom to human nature, but this has been badly harmed by original sin, the sin of humanity.

God gave his grace to Adam and Eve. It was the greatest of his gifts to them because they shared in the very life of God. They were truly free with the freedom of children of God. Through sin, however, the human race lost God's life, the life of grace. Even our freedom was badly harmed by original sin, the sin of humanity.

133. How is human weakness overcome?

Human weakness after original sin is overcome by grace, so that we can live with holiness in the faith of Jesus Christ.

Our hope lies in the grace of Jesus Christ, merited for us by his Death on the Cross. The freedom of fallen humanity has been so weakened that we would be unable for long to fulfill our duties to God and our neighbor without the help of God's grace. Our freedom is so raised and strengthened that we can live a life pleasing to God in the faith of Jesus Christ.

134. Why does the Church promote human freedom?

The Church promotes human freedom for (1) our welfare on earth and (2) the higher good of grace and eternal salvation.

(1) The Church tries to promote true freedom for our good on earth, defends freedom against unjust force, and asks Christians to work together to protect freedom.

(2) But the Church especially defends freedom for our spiritual welfare. The Church claims that our answer to God in faith must be free. We are not to be forced to accept the Christian faith against our own will. The Church claims freedom for itself as a society of those who have the right to live according to the Christian faith, which leads to their welfare on earth and eternal salvation in heaven.

A. FILL IN THE BLANKS

1. God's plan concerning freedom is that we, united with Jesus Christ, ... (131)
2. At the beginning, God gave the gift of freedom to human nature, but this has been badly harmed by ...., the sin of .... (132)
3. Human weakness after original sin is overcome by .... so that we can .... (133)
4. The Church promotes human freedom for (1) .... and (2) .... (134)

B. BIBLE READING

John 15:5-8

The Vine and the Branches

After the Passover supper, Jesus said many things to comfort his beloved disciples before he left them. He had just given them the Eucharist, when he changed bread and wine into his Body and Blood. He told them to do as he did in memory of him, having given them the power to consecrate the bread and wine. To show how closely he would be united with them through the Eucharist he said,

"I am the vine, you are the branches. Whoever abides in me, and I in him, will bear much fruit. Apart from me you can do nothing. Whoever does not abide in me will be thrown away like a withered branch. Such branches are gathered up, thrown into the fire, and burned.

"If you abide in me and my words abide in you, you may ask for whatever you wish, and it will be done for you. By this is my Father glorified, that you bear much fruit and become my disciples."

It is God's plan that, united with Jesus, we willingly do God's will. By the grace of Jesus we can overcome our human weakness. His grace is like the sap that goes through the vine into the branches to give them life and strength. Jesus is the vine, and we are the branches.

Discussion:

1. When did Jesus speak these words?
2. Who is the vine and who are the branches?
3. What will happen if we are united with Jesus, the vine?
4. What will happen if we do not remain united with Jesus?
5. What does Jesus promise through our prayers if we remain with him?
6. Can we overcome our human weaknesses without the grace of Christ?

C. PRACTICE

1. God is always offering us actual graces, that is, the help we need to do good and to avoid evil. He gives us light for our minds and strength for our wills. Each day we should pray that we may make good use of his graces. God sends us these graces in order that we may do good deeds that will make God's life grow in our souls. Since we are free to accept or refuse these graces, we should pray that we may use God's graces well and in this way answer his call.
2. The Holy Spirit, who dwells in our soul as in a temple, is the giver of light and strength. We should often pray to him that he may change us as he changed the apostles on Pentecost. We shall then be true witnesses of Jesus Christ.

CHAPTER
21 The Moral Life of Christians

135. If we are to answer God's love, what must we do?

If we are to answer God's love, we must (1) observe everything that Christ has commanded and (2) believe all that he has taught.

(1) The teaching of the Church includes all those things that are to be done or avoided in order that the followers of Jesus might live the Christian life according to his will. If we truly love God, we shall try to do his holy will in everything.

(2) The teaching of the Church includes all the truths of faith that Jesus taught. Before ascending into heaven Jesus said, "Teach them to observe all that I have commanded you" (Mt 28:20).

136. What does Christian morality teach?

Christian morality teaches us a way of living a life worthy of a human being and of an adopted child of God so that we may grow in the new life given to us through Jesus Christ.

Christian morality shows us a way of life worthy of a human being and a child of God so that we may grow in the grace and love of God. The Church teaches: "The object, the intention, and the circumstances make up the three 'sources' of the morality of human acts" (CCC 1757). Furthermore, the Church teaches: "A morally good act requires the goodness of its object, of its end, and of its circumstances together" (CCC 1760).

137. How is Christian morality supported and guided?

Christian morality is supported and guided by the grace and gifts of the Holy Spirit.

So that we may live well as God's children, the Holy Spirit helps us to respect each other because united in Christ we share his life of grace. He gives us the desire and the help we need to do things pleasing to our heavenly Father. He makes clear what Jesus taught us in the Gospel, and helps us to remain true to Jesus and to his Church. These helps of the Holy Spirit are called actual graces. Without these helps it is impossible to do anything toward our own salvation or the salvation of others.

138. What is conscience?

"Conscience is a judgment of reason whereby the human person recognizes the moral quality of a concrete act that he is going to perform, is in the process of performing, or has already completed" (CCC 1778).

Our conscience is our reason judging on moral matters. Our conscience tells us whether an action is right or wrong, a mortal or a venial sin. It guides us in knowing when we act sinfully. Conscience must be formed according to the teachings of Christ and his Church.

139. Must each person have a right conscience?

Each person must have a right conscience and follow it.

The moral life of Christians must be guided by the grace and gifts of the Holy Spirit. We must have a right conscience and follow it.

140. How must a Catholic form a right conscience?

A Catholic must form a right conscience by obeying the teaching authority of God's Church.

We do not always know whether our conscience is right. But we can train our conscience by listening to the Word of God in the Gospels and in the Church and by being attentive to the inspiration of the Holy Spirit within us.

141. What does obedience to the Holy Spirit include?

Obedience to the Holy Spirit includes a faithful observance of (1) the commandments of God, (2) the laws of the Church, and (3) just civil laws.

We should let the Holy Spirit guide us. He will bend our wills and touch our hearts if we will let him. We ought to pray each day for the strength to say yes to what the Spirit wants to do in us. Obedience to him includes a faithful observance of (1) the commandments of God, (2) the laws of the Church, and (3) just civil laws.

A. FILL IN THE BLANKS

1. If we are to answer God's love, we must (1) ....(2) and .... (135)
2. Christian morality teaches us .... worthy of .... and of .... so that we may grow in .... given to us through .... (136)
3. Christian morality is supported and guided by ....(137)
4. "Conscience is .... whereby the human person recognizes the .... of a concrete act that he ...., is in the process of ...., or has ...."(138)
5. Each person must have a.......... conscience and ....it. (139)
6. A Catholic must form a right conscience by ....(140)
7. Obedience to the Holy Spirit includes a faithful observance of (1) ...., (2) the laws of ...., and (3) ....(141)

B. BIBLE READING

Matthew 28:16-20
Luke 24:50-53

The Last Instruction and Ascension of Jesus

[Forty days after the Resurrection,] the eleven disciples set out for Galilee, to the mountain where Jesus had told them to meet him. When they saw him, they prostrated themselves before him, although some doubted. Then Jesus approached them and said, "All authority in heaven and on earth has been given to me. Go, therefore, and make disciples of all nations, baptizing them in the name of the Father and of the Son and of the Holy Spirit, and teaching them to observe all that I have commanded you. And behold, I am with you always, to the end of the world."

Then he led them out as far as Bethany, and lifting up his hands he blessed them. While he was blessing them, he departed from them and was taken up to heaven. They worshiped him and then returned to Jerusalem filled with great joy, and they were continually in the temple praising God.

"I am with you always, to the end of the world."

Discussion:

1. Where did Jesus meet his followers forty days after the Resurrection?
2. What did Jesus say to his apostles?
3. When he told them to observe all he had commanded them, what did he mean?
4. What did Jesus mean when he said that he would be with them always?
5. What did Jesus do after he gave his last instruction?
6. What did the apostles do after Jesus was taken up to heaven?

C. PRACTICE

1. The kind of happiness that Jesus Christ promises in this life comes from loving God and being loved by God, and from the hope of eternal happiness in heaven. Jesus did not promise us pleasure or wealth. He tells us that it is only through suffering and self-sacrifice that we can have joy and peace of soul in this life. He has not only told us how to live, but he has shown us by his example. What is more, he gives us all the help we need to follow his example. We should, therefore, learn to know and love Jesus Christ. We can do so by frequently reading the Gospels and studying the teaching of the Church about what we must believe and how we must observe what Jesus has commanded.
2. If we love Christ and try to follow his example we shall receive the strength he promised, especially in the Sacrament of the Holy Eucharist and in prayer.

JESUS SPEAKS:

"I give you a new commandment: love one another. Just as I have loved you, so you should also love one another. This is how everyone will know that you are my disciples: if you love one another." (Jn 13:34-35)

"The command I give you is this: love one another." (Jn 15:17)

Holiness means being in love with God

CHAPTER

22 Perfect Christian Love

142. In what are all commandments summed up?

All commandments are summed up in faith working through love.

The moral teaching of Jesus is summed up in the two commandments he gave his Church: "You shall love the Lord your God with all your heart, and with all your soul, and with all your mind, and with all your strength. . . . You shall love your neighbor as yourself" (Mk 12:30-31). Other words and the example of Jesus tell of how these commandments are to be practiced.

143. What is our greatest responsibility?

Our greatest responsibility is to do God's will by (1) keeping his commandments and living in his love and (2) practicing the "new commandment" of love of neighbor.

(1) Jesus said, "As the Father has loved me, so have I loved you. Remain in my love. If you keep my commandments, you will remain in my love, just as I have kept my Father's commandments and remain in his love" (Jn 15:9-10).

(2) One can tell true Christians by the love they show for others. Jesus said, "I give you a new commandment: love one another. Just as I have loved you, so you should also love one another. This is how everyone will know that you are my disciples: if you love one another" (Jn 13:34-35).

144. What is a person's holiness?

A person's holiness, whatever his or her state of life may be, is perfect love of God.

The life of Jesus shows us in a human way that God's life is a life of love. Father, Son, and Holy Spirit are forever giving themselves to each other.

God asks us to be holy. To be holy is being like God. This means sharing more and more of our life with him so that he can finish the good work he began in us through his grace in Baptism, when we first received his divine life and became his children. Jesus said, "Therefore, strive to be perfect, just as your heavenly Father is perfect" (Mt 5:48). Our holiness is perfect love of God.

145. Why is love of God the soul of morality?

Love of God is the soul of morality because God is love, and in God's plan that love reaches out in Jesus Christ, to unite us in our love for one another.

(1) God loves us. He always has loved us and always will love us. He watches over us every moment of our lives. He gave us all the good things in life that we have, including life, health, family, and friends. God made us his children in Baptism and promised to grant us eternal life with him in heaven, if we are faithful to him.

(2) God's love reaches us through Jesus. In his perfect love for us, Jesus died on the Cross to make up for our personal sins and regain for us the life of grace and eternal life with God. By means of his personal presence and the gift of sanctifying grace, the Holy Spirit makes us pleasing to God and holy. He makes us children in the family of God and unites us in faith and love to Christ and to each other. St. John says, "Beloved, let us love one another, because love is from God. Everyone who loves is born of God and knows God. Whoever does not love does not know God, because God is love" (1 Jn 4:7-8).

146. Why do men and women accept a religious vocation?

Men and women accept a religious vocation to show in this special and needed way their love of God and true service to others.

The perfection of Christian life consists in love: first in the love of God, then in the love of neighbor. The whole life of a religious is to be one continuous act of love in the service of God and the Church. "Christ proposes the evangelical counsels [poverty, chastity, and obedience], in their great variety, to every disciple.... It is the *profession* of these counsels, within a permanent state of life recognized by the Church, that characterizes the life consecrated to God" (CCC 915).

A. FILL IN THE BLANKS

1. All commandments are summed up in ....(142)
2. Our greatest responsibility is .... by (1) .... and (2) .... (143)
3. A person's holiness is .... (144)
4. Love of God is the soul of morality because ...., and in God's plan that love reaches out in ...., to unite us in .... (145)
5. Men and women accept a religious vocation to .... (146)

B. BIBLE READING Luke 10:25-37

The Good Samaritan

A lawyer came forward to test Jesus by asking, "Teacher, what must I do to gain eternal life?"

Jesus said to him, "What is written in the Law? How do you read it?"

He answered, "You shall love the Lord your God with all your heart, and with all your soul, and with all your strength, and with all your mind, and your neighbor as yourself."

Jesus then said to him, "You have answered correctly. Do this and you will live."

The Good Samaritan

But because the man wished to justify himself, he asked, "And who is my neighbor?"

Jesus replied, "A man was going down from Jerusalem to Jericho, when he was attacked by robbers. They stripped him and beat him, and then went off leaving him half-dead. A priest happened to be traveling along that same road, but when he saw him he passed by on the other side. A Levite likewise came to that spot and saw him, but he too passed by on the other side.

"But a Samaritan who was traveling along that road came upon him, and when he saw him he was moved with compassion. He went up to him and bandaged his wounds after having poured oil and wine on them. Then he brought him upon his own animal to an inn and looked after him.

"The next day, he took out two denarii [coins] and gave them to the innkeeper, saying, 'Look after him, and when I return I will repay you for anything more you might spend.'

"Which of those three, do you think, was a neighbor to the man who fell into the hands of the robbers?" He answered, "The one who showed him mercy." Jesus said to him, "Go and do likewise."

Discussion:

1. What did the lawyer want to know?
2. What did the lawyer say was written in the Law?
3. What did the priest and the Levite do when they saw the man who was attacked by robbers?
4. What did the Samaritan do when he found the man who was robbed?
5. What did Jesus tell the lawyer to do?
6. How does this story explain perfect Christian love?

C. PRACTICE

1. We have been made children of God, for in Baptism we received a new life from Christ. We must therefore live a new life according to the dignity of a Christian. The Christian life is a life of love. We would not be able to love God or one another as children of God without a special gift from him, the gift of charity. This gift is one of the great powers that God gives us with the gift of the divine life: the power to believe God, the power to hope in him, and the power to love him and our neighbor as children of God. These gifts—together with the gifts of the Holy Spirit and other helps that God gives us—help us to live according to the new life as members of the Mystical Body of Christ. Our one aim in life should be to practice our faith in God through love. This means that we should love God above all things for his own sake and to love ourselves and others as children of God for his sake.
2. We express love for our neighbors by treating them with the reverence they deserve as children of God. We must treat everyone as we would treat Christ himself. We must practice the works of mercy.

JESUS SPEAKS:

"No one can have greater love than to lay down his life for his friends." (Jn 15:13)

CHAPTER 23 Duties Flowing from Love of God and Others

147. How do we know the duties flowing from love of God and others?

We know the duties flowing from love of God and others from (1) the Ten Commandments of God; (2) the Sermon on the Mount, especially the Beatitudes; (3) the spiritual and corporal works of mercy; (4) the virtues and seven capital sins; and (5) the laws of the Church.

(1) The *Ten Commandments* constitute an important part of the message of salvation to Moses. Like the first People of God we Christians accept the commandments as a part of our agreement of faithfulness to God. By keeping the commandments we give ourselves to God in loving obedience. All the commandments are contained in the two commandments of love of God and neighbor.

(2) The *Beatitudes* express some of the high standards of Christ's kingdom and the reward promised for living according to them.

(3) The *spiritual works of mercy* are these: correct the sinner, instruct the ignorant, advise the doubtful, comfort the sorrowful, bear wrongs patiently, forgive all injuries, and pray for the living

and the dead. The *corporal works of mercy* are these: feed the hungry, give drink to the thirsty, clothe the naked, visit the imprisoned, shelter the homeless, visit the sick, and bury the dead.

(4) The *virtues* that concern God (theological) are faith, hope, and charity. Those that concern man (moral) are prudence, justice, fortitude, and temperance.

(5) The *laws of the Church* are some duties expected of Catholic Christians today.

148. What are our duties toward God?

(1) The will of God must be put first in our lives. (2) We must act as children toward God, our all-good and all-loving Father, and never try to live apart from him. (3) We must gladly give God true worship and prayer.

God's will must be our first priority. As his children, we are to love him, obey him, and thank him for being our all-good and all-loving Father. We must worship him at Holy Mass and with our prayer and devotion.

149. How do we sin against the honor due to God?

Idolatry is to put someone or something in place of God; blasphemy is to dishonor God by our words.

(1) This is the *First Commandment:* "I, the Lord, am your God. You shall not have other gods besides me." It binds us to adoration. It warns us against any action that would lead us away from the true adoration of the living God: neglect to learn the truths God has taught, or refusal to believe these truths; leaving God's Church; giving in to superstitious practices.

(2) This is the *Second Commandment:* "You shall not take the name of the Lord, your God, in vain." We must have respect for God's name and everything connected with it. We honor God's name by invoking God in our prayers and Holy Mass.

(3) This is the *Third Commandment:* "Remember to keep holy the Sabbath." We are obliged to attend Mass each Sunday (or Saturday evening) and holyday of obligation. The Mass is the highest form of worship. Sunday is a weekly reminder of our Lord's Easter victory and of the joy that God's people share with Christ. By resting from our usual work, we find it easier to join with other Christians in making Sunday a day of thanks for the triumph of Jesus Christ.

150. What are our duties toward others?

Like Christ, (1) we must show our love for others by concern for their rights; (2) we must reach out to help others; (3) our thoughts and words concerning others must be ruled by the love we owe the children of God; and (4) we must respect and obey all lawful authority in the home, in society, and in the Church.

(1) Immediately beside the great law of the kingdom of God, "You shall love the Lord your God with all your heart," there is the command "and your neighbor as yourself" (Lk 10:27). The commandment of love of neighbor found in the Old Testament is carried over into the new law, where it is renewed. Jesus declared that this commandment of fraternal love is his favorite and his own commandment. "This is my commandment: love one another as I have loved you" (Jn 15:12). This love is the sign by which his disciples will be clearly recognized.

Today we are challenged to live our life in such a way that we will bear witness to God by serving the needs of others. As Christians, we can serve others by personally taking care of their spiritual, physical, and social needs—their freedom, housing, food, health, and right to work, among others.

(2) We must bring our Christian faith into a way of life based on the spirit of the gospel. This is the Christian life. The Church urges us to serve God by serving others after the example of Jesus Christ. Christians must be servants because Jesus was. Such a life calls for sacrifice and earnest effort. The Church wants

us to have room in our hearts for all people so that we might labor with them to build up human society. We do this by reaching out to help others. A life of service to others is the best way of letting people know that God is present in the world and that he loves all of us.

(3) God commands us to think kindly. Jesus said, "Do not judge, so that you in turn may not be judged" (Mt 7:1). Kindness excludes evil and suspicious thoughts.

Our speech concerning others must also be ruled by love. The sin of uncharitable talk destroys unity within any family. It violates truth, justice, and love.

(4) This is the *Fourth Commandment:* "Honor your father and your mother." Authority is the right, power, and duty to govern the members of a family, the members of the Church, or the citizens of a country. All authority comes from God. The authority of parents is from God. Even the authority of the government comes from God. We who are members of the Mystical Body of Christ are to imitate the reverence that he showed for those in authority. We are commanded especially to give our parents respect and love. As children, we owe them obedience.

151. How do we sin against others?

We sin against others when we (1) show little interest in helping meet their needs; (2) steal, damage others' good name or property, cheat, or fail to pay our debts; (3) show anger and hatred; and (4) are immodest in behavior and dress.

(1) It is sinful to be so selfish as to show no interest in helping others. Jesus reminded us that what we do for others we do for him.

(2) This is the *Seventh Commandment:* "You shall not steal." This is the *Tenth Commandment:* "You shall not covet your neighbor's goods." All the goods of this world came from a

good God. Material goods that God gives us are not for ourselves alone; they also are for our family and others in need. The Seventh and Tenth Commandments forbid us to take something that belongs to another without permission. Stealing, damaging the property of another, not paying just debts, wasting the money or property of an employer, and depriving our family of needed money by drinking or foolish spending are all sins against these two commandments.

This is the ***Eighth Commandment:*** "You shall not bear false witness against your neighbor." A good name is the esteem with which a person is held by others. To harm a person's good name is a sin both when the unkind talk is based on truth (detraction) and when it is based on a lie (calumny). Revealing a person's hidden faults and gossiping about a person's known faults are ways of damaging a person's reputation. Telling a lie is never permitted.

(3) This is the ***Fifth Commandment:*** "You shall not kill." This commandment directs us to care for our body, mind, and soul and to care for the body and soul of our neighbor. We must practice self-discipline in the use of food, alcohol, tobacco, and drugs. Christ's followers are to oppose whatever may destroy or abuse human life. This commandment also forbids unjust anger, which leads to hatred, revenge, fighting, and quarreling.

(4) This is the ***Sixth Commandment:*** "You shall not commit adultery." This is the ***Ninth Commandment:*** "You shall not covet your neighbor's wife." The sexual passion, implanted in us by God as a sacred power, is something *holy*. It is *important* in God's plan of creation and providence. Its misuse is sinful. The full use of the sexual passion is a right and privilege of those who are validly married.

Sins against these commandments are adultery, fornication, and self-abuse. Though it is impossible to keep all evil thoughts and desires from our minds, we can, at least, refuse to give them a welcome. Unwelcome desires, no matter how wrong they seem, cannot defile our heart.

152. What are our duties toward self?

We must (1) be an example of Christian goodness; (2) be humble and patient with ourselves and others; (3) be simple in the use of the things of this world; (4) be pure in words and actions; and (5) avoid pride, laziness, envy, and intemperance in food and drink.

(1) No one has ever given of self for others as much as Jesus did when he lived among us. We Christians should try to imitate the love of Jesus in such a way that others will want to copy it. By our example of kindness to others, we can spread our faith.

(2) The true way to holiness is to love God and our neighbor for God's sake and to sacrifice ourselves in order to fulfill the great commandment of love. Our patience in our shortcomings and those of others pleases God.

(3) By the example of their spirit of simplicity in using the things of this world, Christians can bear witness to the teaching of Christ in a world so taken up with material things.

(4) In today's world, where the body and sensuality count for so much, the true Christian life of decency in word and action proves that purity is possible and pleasing to God. It gives us greater freedom to serve the needs of others.

(5) If we pray, God will always give us strength to overcome temptation. In order to avoid sin we must also avoid any person, place, or thing that will lead us into sin. We should pray in particular for the grace to guard against such capital sins as pride, greed, envy, and anger because they give rise to other sins.

A. FILL IN THE BLANKS

1. We know the duties flowing from love of God and man from (1) ....; (2) ....; (3) ....; (4) ....; and (5) .... (147)

2. Our duties toward God: (1) ....must be put first in our lives. (2) We must act as ...., our all-good and all-loving Father, and never try to .... (3) We must gladly give God .... (148)
3. Idolatry is to ....; blasphemy is to ....(149)
4. Our duties toward others: Like Christ, (1) we must show our love for others by ....; (2) we must reach out to ....; (3) our thoughts and words concerning others must ruled by ....; and (4) we must .... all lawful authority in the ...., in ...., and in .... (150)
5. We sin against others when we (1) show little interest ....; (2) steal, damage others' .... cheat, or fail to pay ....; (3) show ....; and (4) are immodest in .... (151)
6. Our duties toward self: We must (1) be an example of ....; (2) be humble and patient with ....; (3) be simple in the use of ....; (4) be pure in ....; and (5) avoid .... (152)

B. BIBLE READING Exodus 20:1-17; 32; 33; 34

The Ten Commandments

Moses brought the people out from the camp to the foot of Mount Sinai. On the morning of the third day there was thunder and lightning. All the mountain shook and gave out smoke like a furnace. A trumpet sounded loudly. God began to speak from the cloud.

"I am the LORD, your God. You shall not have other gods instead of me.

"You shall not take the name of the LORD, your God, in vain.

"Remember the Sabbath and keep it holy.

"Honor your father and your mother.

"You shall not kill.

"You shall not commit adultery.

"You shall not steal.

"You shall not give false witness against your neighbor.

"You shall not covet your neighbor's wife.

Moses destroys the stone tablets and the golden calf.

"You shall not covet anything that belongs to your neighbor."

Moses approached the dark cloud where God was found, and he remained with the Lord for forty days and forty nights. At the end of this time, God gave Moses two stone tablets on which God himself had written the Ten Commandments.

The people became tired waiting for Moses. They went to Aaron and said, "Make a god to walk before us."

Aaron answered them, "Bring your gold earnings to me." He melted the gold, and from the metal he shaped an image of a calf.

Moses prayed to God to spare the people. When he came down the mountain and saw the golden calf and the people singing and dancing around it, he was very angry. He threw down the tablets of stone and broke them at the foot of the mountain. The gold calf he burned and ground into powder.

The next day, Moses went up Mount Sinai to obtain pardon for the sin of the people.

God told Moses to make two tablets of stone like the first ones he had broken. God again wrote the Ten Commandments on them.

Discussion:

1. What happened on Mount Sinai before God began to speak from the cloud?
2. What are the first three commandments of God that are about him?
3. What are the fourth to the tenth commandments that are about our neighbor?
4. How long was Moses with the Lord?
5. What did the people do while Moses was on the mountain?
6. What did Moses do when he returned from the mountain?
7. Why did Moses return to the mountain?
8. Must we keep these same commandments today?

C. PRACTICE

1. We cannot love someone we do not know. God has told us of himself in order that we might love him. Because we are God's children, we know God more than those who do not have the gift of faith. We can gain more knowledge of our faith by reading and study. Studying our religion faithfully is a sign of our love for God. It also is an important way of loving him even more. By loving and serving God, we can lead others to know him better because our good example does more good than words. We displease God by not caring to know more about him. By our bad example, we may be keeping others from loving him more.
2. Chastity is a virtue that is important to man and woman. Sex is something good and holy. There is nothing evil about any part of the body, but it is important to understand that the sexual power

is to be used only in marriage. It is a means of cooperating with God in bringing children into the world. The misuse of sex (outside of marriage and even within marriage) is something contrary to God's will because sex as a gift from him is something sacred. It is a sin against all forms of love: human love, the love of God (as is every sin), and also the love of our neighbor because we are leading another person into sin.

Chastity and modesty are complementary virtues that preserve a person's dignity. "The chaste person maintains the integrity of the powers of life and love placed in him. This integrity ensures the unity of the person; it is opposed to any behavior that would impair it. It tolerates neither a double life nor duplicity in speech" (CCC 2338).

"Modesty protects the intimate center of the person. It means refusing to unveil what should remain hidden.... It guides how one looks at others and behaves toward them in conformity with the dignity of persons and their solidarity" (CCC 2521).

Embracing these virtues encourages a sense of self-worth and an understanding of the value of others. Self-respect and respect for others will enable true, honest, and uplifting relationships in the face of the world's insistence on defiling human sexuality.

JESUS SPEAKS:

"You shall love the Lord your God with all your heart, and with all your soul, and with all your strength, and with all your mind, and your neighbor as yourself." (Lk 10:27)

"Anyone who has received my commandments and observes them is the one who loves me. And whoever loves me will be loved by my Father, and I will love him and reveal myself to him." (Jn 14:21)

"If you keep my commandments, you will remain in my love, just as I have kept my Father's commandments and remain in his love." (Jn 15:10)

"Whoever loves me will keep my word, and my Father will love him, and we will come to him and make our abode with him." (Jn 14:23)

Part Ten — MARY AND THE SAINTS

CHAPTER 24 Mary, Mother of God, Mother and Model of the Church

153. Why is Mary in the Church in a place highest after Christ?

Mary is in the Church in a place highest after Christ because she is (1) the ever-virgin Mother of Jesus Christ, our Lord and God and (2) very close to us as our spiritual Mother.

(1) Mary is in the Church in a place highest after Christ because she is the Mother of God. An angel had come to ask her consent to God's wish that she become the Mother of his Son. She not only consented, she also willed to be his Mother and to have an important part in his mission of saving the world.

(2) At the Incarnation at Nazareth, Mary gave Jesus to us. On Calvary, Jesus gave us his Mother. In becoming the Mother of God, she also willed to become our spiritual Mother. Through her prayers to her Son we hope to reach salvation.

154. What are some of the special gifts Mary received from God?

Some of the special gifts Mary received from God are these: (1) being Mother of God, (2) being preserved from all stain of original sin, and (3) being taken body and soul to heaven.

(1) The Blessed Virgin worked together with the Divine Word, the Son of God, and with the Holy Spirit in the great work of the Incarnation. She is the Mother of God, and this is the reason for all her power before God and for her holiness.

(2) In view of the merits of her Divine Son, Mary alone enjoyed the privilege of being preserved from original sin. Mary was never subject to the evil spirit. She was always in the state of sanctifying grace.

(3) After a most blessed death, Mary was assumed body and soul into heaven and was crowned Queen of Heaven by her own Son.

155. What veneration do we owe to Mary?

We owe special veneration by word and example to Mary as Mother of Christ, Mother of the Church, and our spiritual Mother.

The Church urges us to give special veneration to Mary who is the Mother of God, the Mother of the Church, and our spiritual Mother as well. In doing this we imitate her Son who loved and honored his Mother more than any other human being. He made her holier and more beautiful than any other member of his Church, for she is truly the Mother of the Church. By following her example and by seeking her help in prayer we can be sure of reaching her Son in eternal life.

156. Why does the Church honor the other saints?

The Church honors the other saints who are already with the Lord in heaven because (1) they inspire us by the good example of their lives and (2) we ask them to pray to God for us.

(1) Because of our union with Christ, we are united with all those who share his life in the larger family of God, the Communion of Saints. We honor the saints when we try to imitate the example of their virtuous lives.

(2) We honor them also when we pray to them. We on earth (Church Militant) are helped by the prayers of the victorious and blessed members of the family in heaven (Church Triumphant). We also share in their merits gained by their holy lives.

157. What is our duty toward the deceased?

We must (1) have reverence toward the bodies of those who have gone before us in death and (2) pray for deceased relatives, friends, and all the faithful departed.

(1) We show respect for the bodies of the deceased because they were temples of the Holy Spirit and are destined to rise gloriously.

(2) We can help the members of God's family whose souls are being purified in purgatory (Church Suffering). They can and do pray for us, even though they cannot help themselves. Through the Communion of Saints we are one with loved ones, friends, and all who rest in Christ.

A. FILL IN THE BLANKS

1. Mary is in the Church in a place highest after Christ because she is (1) .... and (2) ....(153)
2. Some of the special gifts Mary received from God are these: (1) being ...., (2) being ...., ...(3) and being ....(154)

3. We owe special veneration by word and example to Mary as ...., ..., and .... (155)
4. The Church honors the other saints who are already with the Lord in heaven because (1) .... and (2) .... (156)
5. We must (1) ....toward the bodies of those who have gone before us in death and (2) ....(157)

B. BIBLE READING

Luke 1:26-38

The Annunciation

The hour was at hand for which God had been preparing his people. The world was looking for a Redeemer. The Jews prayed that God would now keep the promise he made to Adam and Eve and had repeated again and again through the prophets.

The angel Gabriel was sent by God to a town in Galilee called Nazareth, to a virgin betrothed to a man named Joseph, of the house of David. The virgin's name was Mary. The angel came to her and said, "Hail, full of grace! The Lord is with you."

But she was greatly troubled by his words and wondered in her heart what this salutation could mean. Then the angel said to her, "Do not be afraid, Mary, for you have found favor with God. Behold, you will conceive in your womb and bear a son, and you will name him Jesus. He will be great and will be called Son of the Most High. The Lord God will give him the throne of his ancestor David. He will rule over the house of Jacob forever, and of his kingdom there will be no end."

Mary said to the angel, "How will this be, since I am a virgin?" The angel answered, "The Holy Spirit will come upon you, and the power of the Most High will overshadow you. Therefore, the child to be born will be holy, and he will be called the Son of God. And behold, your cousin Elizabeth in her old age has also conceived a son, and she who was called barren is now in her sixth month, for nothing will be impossible for God."

Then Mary said, "Behold, I am the servant of the Lord. Let it be done to me according to your word." After this, the angel departed from her.

As soon as Mary gave this answer, she became the Mother of God. The Second Person of the Blessed Trinity took to himself a body and soul like ours. He became Man and dwelt among us. This is called the mystery of the Incarnation. Mary is truly the Mother of God.

Discussion:

1. Who was Mary?
2. Who was Joseph?
3. What did the angel say to Mary?
4. Why did the angel say that Mary did not have to be afraid?
5. How did the angel say everything would happen?
6. What was Mary's answer to the angel?
7. What happened when Mary gave her answer?
8. Why is Mary the Mother of God?

C. PRACTICE

1. The devotion to our Blessed Mother that is especially dear to her and to her children is the Rosary. The Hail Marys that we recite as we meditate on the mysteries of the life of Jesus and Mary are a means of expressing our love for them. We should make an effort to say the Rosary each day. The Blessed Virgin herself requested that we say the Rosary when she appeared to St. Bernadette at Lourdes in France and to the three children at Fatima in Portugal.

Part Eleven — DEATH, JUDGMENT, ETERNITY

CHAPTER 25 Final Reunion with God

158. Why should we face death with courage and joy?

We have reason to live and to face death with courage and joy because (1) the Lord's Resurrection means that death has been conquered; (2) in the risen Christ we live, we die, and we shall live again; and (3) we look ahead to a coming home to God, our loving Father.

(1) Death is the separation of body and soul from each other. We believe that death is the passage over the doorway of earthly life to the life beyond. Jesus gave death a new meaning, changing it into an event that brought salvation. He did this by becoming Man and taking death on himself. In his Death Jesus gave himself as a perfect sacrifice to the heavenly Father. As the second Adam, by his glorious Resurrection Jesus gained his final victory over the lord of death.

(2) The Resurrection of Christ is the most important proof of our resurrection in the body. Through the merits of his Son, God has set up his new order, according to which Jesus is to be the beginning of resurrection. St. Paul said, "Since death came into the world through a man, the resurrection of the dead has also come through a man. Just as in Adam all die, so all will be brought to life in Christ" (1 Cor 15:21-22).

(3) We should face death with courage and joy, looking ahead to coming home to God, our loving Father. God made us for himself. Our highest happiness will be to be united with him forever in heaven, our true home.

159. What will happen when Christ returns with power?

When Christ returns with power as judge of the living and the dead, he will hand over his people to the Father.

Jesus prophesied that he would return to earth one day in triumph to judge the living and the dead. His enemies will be forever conquered, and he will bring history to its appointed end.

160. Until the Lord's arrival in majesty, where will his disciples be?

Until the Lord's arrival in majesty, (1) some of his disciples are pilgrims on earth; (2) some have finished this life and are being purified in purgatory; and (3) others are in glory, beholding God himself.

(1) Some of our Lord's disciples are pilgrims on earth, journeying toward their heavenly homeland.

(2) At the very instant the soul leaves the body it is judged by Almighty God. This judgment is called the Particular Judgment. If we die without the least trace of sin upon our soul, the immediate sight of God in heaven will itself be our judgment.

Anyone who dies in the grace of God but is not free from all sins and all punishment due for sins cannot go to heaven at once.

Those who still have to do penance for their sins go first to a place of cleansing that we call purgatory ("cleansing place").

(3) The beatific vision is an immediate vision of God. This person-to-person union with him is the happiness of heaven. The full flowering of supernatural life to which God in his mercy raised us is the future eternal life. This happiness for which man was created is everlasting.

161. What will happen on the day of the Last Judgment?

On the day of the Last Judgment, each of us will reach his or her eternal destiny: all of us will be revealed before the judgment place of Christ, so that each one may receive what each deserves, according to what was done on earth, good or bad.

All mankind will be judged at the end of the world by Jesus Christ, not only as God but also as man. Jesus himself taught us that he would be the judge of mankind.

God will reward all according to their works at the Last Judgment, giving eternal life to those who persevere in good works to the end. Our union with God will be so complete that we cannot now even faintly imagine the joy of it. We also shall know our loved ones in heaven.

162. What will happen to evildoers?

Evildoers shall rise to be damned in hell.

Having willingly cut itself off from God during life, the soul that has died without turning back to God has no means by which to get in touch with God. It has lost God forever, having died without that bond of union with God that we call sanctifying grace. Hell is eternal separation from God.

163. What will happen to those who have done right?

Those who have done right shall rise to live a life eternally with God and will receive the good things that he has prepared for those who love him.

We believe that the just who have been made perfect through death and purgatory are now in heaven, though they have not yet risen in the body nor undergone the Last Judgment. We are called to glorify God in heaven in a perfect manner by love and self-surrender to him. God is the highest good that we not only shall know and love, but also live, in a mysterious sharing of his life.

164. What do Christians look forward to during this life?

During this earthly life, Christians look forward to their final reunion with God.

On his return, Jesus will raise from the dead the bodies of those who died in union with him. The Father will raise us up as well because of Jesus, if we turn to the Son in faith. Jesus promised that someday he would raise up all those who had been entrusted to him. By rising from the dead, they will share in his Resurrection in the fullest way. When Jesus has subjected all things to himself, he will deliver his dominion to the Father.

A. FILL IN THE BLANKS

1. We have reason to live and to face death with .... because (1) the Lord's Resurrection means that ....; (2) in the risen Christ we ...., we ...., and we shall ....; and (3) we look ahead to a .... (158)
2. When Christ returns with power as judge of the living and the dead, he will ....(159)
3. Until the Lord's arrival in majesty, (1) some of his disciples are ....; (2) some have finished this life and are ....; and (3) others are .... (160)
4. On the day of the Last Judgment, each of us will reach ....: all of us will be ...., so that each one may receive ...., according to what ....(161)
5. Evildoers shall rise to be .... (162)

6. Those who have done right shall rise to .... and will receive .... that he has prepared for .... (163)
7. During this earthly life, Christians look forward to .... (164)

B. BIBLE READING

Matthew 25:31-46

The Last Judgment

Jesus told his disciples about his Second Coming.

He said, "When the Son of Man comes in his glory, and all the angels with him, then he will sit on the throne of his glory. All the nations will be gathered before him, and he will separate people one from another as a shepherd separates the sheep from the goats. He will place the sheep on his right and the goats on his left.

"Then the King will say to those on his right, 'Come, you who are blessed by my Father, inherit the kingdom prepared for you from the

"When the Son of Man comes in his glory, and all the angels with him, then he will sit on the throne of his glory."

foundation of the world. For I was hungry and you gave me something to eat; I was thirsty and you gave me something to drink; I was a stranger and you welcomed me; I was naked and you clothed me; I was ill and you took care of me; I was in prison and you came to visit me.'

"Then the righteous will say to him, 'Lord, when did we see you hungry and give you something to eat, or thirsty and give you something to drink? When did we see you a stranger and welcome you, or naked and clothe you? When did we see you ill or in prison and come to visit you?' And the King will answer, 'Amen, I say to you, whatever you did for one of the least of these brethren of mine, you did for me.'

"Then he will say to those on his left, 'Depart from me, you accursed, into the eternal fire prepared for the devil and his angels. For I was hungry and you did not give me anything to eat; I was thirsty and you did not give me anything to drink; I was a stranger and you did not welcome me; I was naked and you did not give me any clothing; I was ill and in prison and you did not visit me.'

"Then they will ask him, 'Lord, when did we see you hungry or thirsty or a stranger or naked or ill or in prison and not minister to you?' He will answer them, 'Amen, I say to you, whatever you failed to do for one of the least of these brethren of mine, you failed to do for me.' And they will go away to eternal punishment, but the righteous will enter eternal life."

Discussion:

1. How did Jesus tell his disciples about his Second Coming?
2. What will the King say to those on his right?
3. What will the King answer when they ask when they did all these things?
4. What will the King say to those on his left?
5. What will the King answer when they ask when they saw him in need?
6. What will happen to those on the left?
7. What will happen to those on the right?
8. How does this parable tell of our final union with God?

C. PRACTICE

1. We should prepare ourselves to meet our Savior by trying to lead a holy life and by doing our part in spreading the kingdom of God. At one's death each person gives an account of his or her life. Nothing decided at this final accounting will be changed in the Last Judgment.

2. All the means that will help us to live up to the ideals of Jesus Christ are here for us to use. We have the life-giving Sacraments of Penance and the Holy Eucharist to give us holiness and strength. We should receive them often. In many instances, there is the opportunity to receive the great source of grace and love, the Eucharist, on a daily basis. Attending daily Mass will help us to become more deeply united with Christ and our neighbor. Additionally, we will receive help and encouragement from our union with God in prayer.

   People should be able to see in our lives the proof of our deeper union with God that comes from prayer. They should be able to see that we live by faith, that we are strengthened by hope, and that we practice love of God and our neighbor in our daily life. Keep in mind that we shall share in that final victory of Christ if we remain in union with him throughout our lifetime.

JESUS SPEAKS:

"I am the way, and the truth, and the life. No one comes to the Father except through me. If you know me, then you will know my Father also." (Jn 14:6-7)

"Rejoice and be glad, for your reward will be great in heaven." (Mt 5:12)

"The Son of Man will come with his angels in the glory of his Father, and then he will repay everyone according to what has been done." (Mt 16:27)

APPENDICES

APPENDIX A

THE TEN COMMANDMENTS OF GOD

1. I, the Lord, am your God. You shall not have other gods besides me.
2. You shall not take the name of the Lord, your God, in vain.
3. Remember to keep holy the Sabbath.
4. Honor your father and your mother.
5. You shall not kill.
6. You shall not commit adultery.
7. You shall not steal.
8. You shall not bear false witness against your neighbor.
9. You shall not covet your neighbor's wife.
10. You shall not covet your neighbor's goods.

THE BEATITUDES

1. Blessed are the poor in spirit, for theirs is the kingdom of heaven.
2. Blessed are those who mourn, for they will be comforted.
3. Blessed are the meek, for they will inherit the earth.

4. Blessed are those who hunger and thirst for justice, for they will have their fill.
5. Blessed are the merciful, for they will obtain mercy.
6. Blessed are the pure of heart, for they will see God.
7. Blessed are the peacemakers, for they will be called children of God.
8. Blessed are those who are persecuted in the cause of justice, for theirs is the kingdom of heaven. (Mt 5:3-10)

APPENDIX B

DUTIES OF CATHOLICS

1. To keep holy the day of the Lord's Resurrection: to worship God by participating in Mass every Sunday and Holyday of Obligation:* to avoid those activities that would hinder renewal of soul and body, e.g., needless work and business activities, unnecessary shopping, etc.

2. To lead a sacramental life: to receive Holy Communion frequently and the Sacrament of Penance regularly:
—minimally, to receive the Sacrament of Penance at least once a year (annual confession is obligatory only if serious sin is involved).*
—minimally, to receive Holy Communion at least once a year, between the First Sunday of Lent and the Most Holy Trinity.*

Note:

(Duties traditionally mentioned as Precepts of the Church are marked with an asterisk.)

The traditionally listed chief Precepts of the Church are the following six:

1. To assist at Mass on all Sundays and Holydays of Obligation.
2. To fast and abstain on the days appointed.
3. To confess our sins at least once a year.
4. To receive Holy Communion during Easter Time.
5. To contribute to the support of the Church.
6. To observe the laws of the Church concerning marriage.

3. To study Catholic teaching in preparation for the Sacrament of Confirmation, to be confirmed, and then to continue to study and advance the cause of Christ.
4. To observe the marriage laws of the Church:* to give religious training, by example and word, to one's children; to use parish schools and catechetical programs.
5. To strengthen and support the Church:* one's own parish community and parish priests; the worldwide Church and the Holy Father.
6. To do penance, including abstaining from meat and fasting from food on the appointed days.*
7. To join in the missionary spirit and apostolate of the Church.

APPENDIX C

ESSENTIAL PRAYERS

Recommended by the
United States Conference of Catholic Bishops

THE SIGN OF THE CROSS

In the name of the Father, and of the Son, and of the Holy Spirit. Amen.

THE LORD'S PRAYER

OUR Father, who art in heaven, hallowed be Thy name; Thy kingdom come, Thy will be done on earth as it is in heaven. Give us this day our daily bread, and forgive us our trespasses, as we forgive those who trespass against us; and lead us not into temptation, but deliver us from evil. Amen.

HAIL MARY

HAIL, Mary, full of grace! The Lord is with you; blessed are you among women, and blessed is the fruit of your womb, Jesus. Holy Mary, Mother of God, pray for us sinners, now and at the hour of our death. Amen.

THE GLORY BE

GLORY be to the Father, and to the Son, and to the Holy Spirit. As it was in the beginning, is now, and ever shall be, world without end. Amen.

THE APOSTLES' CREED

I BELIEVE in God, the Father Almighty, Creator of heaven and earth, and in Jesus Christ, His only Son, our Lord, Who was conceived by the Holy Spirit, born of the Virgin Mary, suffered under Pontius Pilate, was crucified, died, and was buried; He descended into hell; on the third day He rose again from the dead; He ascended into heaven, and is seated at the right hand of God the Father Almighty; from there He will come to judge the living and the dead. I believe in the Holy Spirit, the holy catholic Church, the Communion of Saints, the forgiveness of sins, the resurrection of the body, and life everlasting. Amen.

ACT OF CONTRITION

O MY God, I am heartily sorry for having offended You, and I detest all my sins, because of Your just punishments, but most of all because they offend You, my God, Who are all good and deserving of all my love. I firmly resolve, with the help of Your grace, to sin no more and to avoid the near occasions of sin. Amen.

ACT OF FAITH

O MY God, I firmly believe that You are one God in three Divine Persons, Father, Son, and Holy Spirit. I believe that Your Divine Son became Man, and died for our sins, and that He will come to judge the living and the dead. I believe these and all the truths that the Holy Catholic Church teaches because You have revealed them, Who can neither deceive nor be deceived.

ACT OF HOPE

O MY God, relying on Your almighty power and infinite mercy and promises, I hope to obtain pardon of my sins, the help of Your grace, and life everlasting, through the merits of Jesus Christ, my Lord and Redeemer.

ACT OF LOVE

O MY God, I love You above all things, with my whole heart and soul, because You are all-good and worthy of all love. I love my neighbor as myself for the love of You. I forgive all who have injured me, and ask pardon of all whom I have injured.

HAIL, HOLY QUEEN

HAIL, holy Queen, Mother of mercy; hail our life, our sweetness, and our hope. To you do we cry, poor banished children of Eve. To you do we send up our sighs, mourning and weeping in this valley of tears. Turn then, most gracious advocate, your eyes of mercy toward us. And after this, our exile, show unto us the blessed fruit of your womb, Jesus. O clement, O loving, O sweet Virgin Mary.

THE HOLY ROSARY

The Five Joyful Mysteries

(Said Mondays and Saturdays [except during Lent] and the Sundays from Advent to Lent)

1. The Annunciation—*Lk 1:26-38*
2. The Visitation—*Lk 1:39-56*
3. The Nativity—*Lk 2:1-7*
4. The Presentation—*Lk 2:22-35*
5. Finding in the Temple—*Lk 2:42-50*

3. THE NATIVITY
For the spirit of poverty.

1. THE ANNUNCIATION
For the love of humility.

4. THE PRESENTATION
For the virtue of obedience.

2. THE VISITATION
For charity toward my neighbor.

5. FINDING IN THE TEMPLE
For the virtue of piety.

THE HOLY ROSARY

1. THE BAPTISM OF JESUS
For keeping Baptismal promises.

The Five Luminous Mysteries*

(Said Thursdays [except during Lent])

1. The Baptism of Jesus—*Mt 3:13-17*
2. Christ's Self-Manifestation at Cana—*Jn 2:1-11*
3. Christ's Proclamation of the Kingdom—*Mk 1:15; Mt 5:1-11*
4. The Transfiguration—*Mt 17:1-8*
5. Institution of the Eucharist—*Mt 26:26*

*Added to the Mysteries of the Rosary by Pope John Paul II in his Apostolic Letter of October 16, 2002, entitled *The Rosary of the Virgin Mary.*

2. CHRIST'S SELF-MANIFESTATION AT CANA
For doing whatever Jesus says.

4. THE TRANSFIGURATION
For becoming a new person in Christ.

3. PROCLAMATION OF THE KINGDOM
For seeking God's forgiveness.

5. INSTITUTION OF THE EUCHARIST
For active participation at Mass.

THE HOLY ROSARY

The Five Sorrowful Mysteries

(Said Tuesdays and Fridays throughout the year and every day during Lent)

1. Agony in the Garden—*Mk 14:35-36*
2. Scourging at the Pillar—*Mk 15:15*
3. Crowning with Thorns—*Mk 15:17*
4. Carrying of the Cross—*Jn 19:17*
5. The Crucifixion—*Lk 23:33*

3. CROWNING WITH THORNS
For moral courage.

1. AGONY IN THE GARDEN
For true contrition.

4. CARRYING OF THE CROSS
For the virtue of patience.

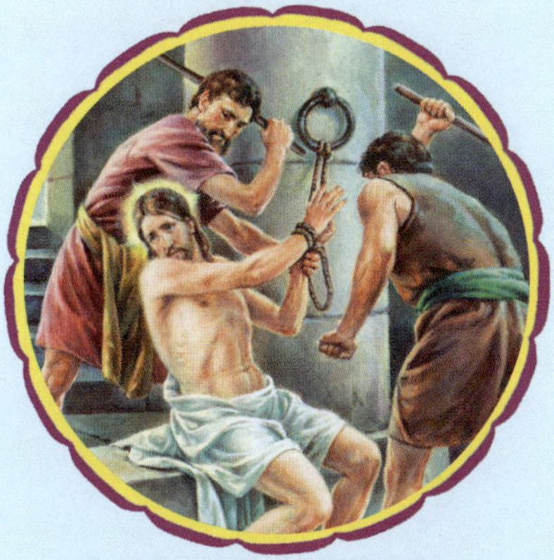

2. SCOURGING AT THE PILLAR
For the virtue of purity.

5. THE CRUCIFIXION
For final perseverance.

THE HOLY ROSARY

The Five Glorious Mysteries

(Said Wednesdays [except during Lent] and for Sundays from Easter until Advent)

1. The Resurrection—***Mk 16:1-7***
2. The Ascension—***Mk 16:19***
3. Descent of the Holy Spirit—***Acts 2:1-4***
4. Assumption of the BVM—***Gen 3:15***
5. Crowning of the BVM—***Rev 12:1***

1. THE RESURRECTION
For the virtue of faith.

2. THE ASCENSION
For the virtue of hope.

3. DESCENT OF THE HOLY SPIRIT
For love of God.

4. ASSUMPTION OF THE BVM
For devotion to Mary.

5. CROWNING OF THE BVM
For eternal happiness.